Samita,
I hope yo
challenged + encou
on this little book
God Bless
Jeff P
:)

I Am Not Jesus,
That's Why I Need Him

A CALL OF T'SHUVA TO AMERICA AND THE NATIONS

by Jeff Pritchard

Scripture references taken from the *Complete Jewish Bible* by David Stern, copyright 1998 by the Jewish New Testament Publications, Inc.

"I Am Not Jesus, That's Why I Need Him," by Jeff Pritchard. ISBN 978-1-60264-561-5.

Published 2010 by Virtualbookworm.com Publishing Inc., P.O. Box 9949, College Station, TX 77842, US. ©2010, Jeff Pritchard. All rights reserved. No part of this publication may be reproduced, stored in a retrieval system, or transmitted in any form or by any means, electronic, mechanical, recording or otherwise, without the prior written permission of Jeff Pritchard.

Manufactured in the United States of America.

TABLE OF CONTENTS

WARNING!

Most of this book was written in 2000 as an encouragement to those who would read it. Much of the "harshness" was not in it. However, after the events of September 11, 2001, I felt compelled to revise it and start with a heart wrenching call to the nations. Over 95% of this book was written by 2003 while George W. Bush was still President. Only minor deletions and updates were made prior to publishing after sitting untouched since 2003. This is a wakeup call to all nations, but it is specifically written to the United States of America.

I hold nothing back, nor do I try to make it easy to swallow. As tempted as I am to try and "tickle your ears," I fear the Living G-d too much to water it down. I am in no way perfect. Far from it. I am not near worthy to untie the shoes of the prophet who claimed to be unworthy to untie the shoes of the Messiah. However, I am obligated as a "redeemed" servant of the Most High to speak what I hear. You may not like my style or my tone of voice, but do not ignore the words of G-d spoken through this imperfect human vessel.

IF you make it through the first two chapters and desire to continue, you will do well. If, however, you refuse to read anymore, then I say to you that you are in no position to neither criticize me nor make comment on this book. For that which follows, comes from the heart of a broken man who has struggled to make sense of the very issues addressed herein. I strongly encourage you to get on your knees and ask for the Creator to give you ears to hear the words in this book and a heart to understand the heart behind them.

With fear and trembling, I urge you to read on...

"How blessed are those who reject the advice of the wicked, don't stand on the way of sinners or sit where scoffers sit! Their delight is in ADONAI'S Torah; on his Torah they meditate day and night. They are like trees planted by streams -- they bear

their fruit in season, their leaves never wither, everything they do succeeds. Not so the wicked, who are like chaff driven by the wind. For this reason the wicked won't stand up to the judgment, nor will sinners at the gathering of the righteous. For ADONAI watches over the way of the righteous, but the way of the wicked is doomed." (Tehillim/Psalms 1)

I AM N.Y. TWINH

I lived up to my name which meant deceiver. I stole my brother's inheritance and lied to my father. Yet, years later, G-d wrestled with me and blessed me. I am N. Y. Twinh. (B'resheet/Genesis 25:19-33:20)

I wanted to burn my daughter-in-law for committing fornication, only to be found guilty for being the cause of her pregnancy. Through the seed of her illegitimate child came the Messiah. I am N. Y. Twinh. (B'resheet/Genesis 38:1-30)

I committed murder while trying to help my people. Later, I wrote five books of the Tenach while communing with G-d face to face. I am N. Y. Twinh. (Sh'mot/Exodus 2:11-15)

I committed adultery with the wife of a man that I later had murdered. I did many other things that displeased my Lord. I also wrote many of the Psalms and was considered by G-d as a man after his own heart. I am N. Y. Twinh. (Sh'mu'el Bet/2 Samuel 11:1-12:23)

I suffered from depression and wanted to die even after calling down fire from heaven and defeating my enemies. I am N. Y. Twinh. (M'lakhim Alef/I Kings 18:1-19:8)

I cheated my own people out of their money and abandoned my dearest friend in his time of need, yet I had the honor of writing his story for multitudes to read. I am N. Y. Twinh. (Mark 2:13-17)

I had five failed marriages and was living in sin with a sixth man when I was allowed to drink of the Living Water. I am N. Y. Twinh. (Yochanan/John 4:1-42)

I hunted innocent people and had them killed. While I was seeking their destruction, I was shown Grace and chosen for another purpose. I am N. Y. Twinh. (Acts 9:1-31)

I was a leader of my people and had great knowledge. I "kept the law" and was of great reputation among my peers. Yet,

something was missing in my life. I am N. Y. Twinh.
(Yochanan/John 3:1-21)

My name is N. Y. Twinh. I am fairly average. I'm not a superstar. I haven't won the Pulitzer. I've made my share of mistakes and have lots of regrets that haunt me. I know I can not measure up to standards that many impose upon even the politicians, or at least, like they used to.

I can not measure up to my own standards. I am very hard on myself. I used to be even harder. But, as I grow older, I find my standards have lowered somewhat. After so many failures in my own eyes, what's the sense? But, surely I'm good enough to get into heaven. Or am I?

Some believe that a suicide mission to kill their enemies assures them a place in paradise or heaven. Some believe that if your good outweighs your bad, that you might get put on the waiting list for heaven. Some believe in nothing and say this life is all there is.

This is heaven? If I kill, I can go to heaven? If I'm just "more good" than I am bad, I might make it in? Woe is me, a sinner! Who will rescue me from this chaos and futility?

I must turn to a source now that I cannot ignore. For in my times of searching, I found that no other place has the answers to my questions. I looked at myself in the mirror. I did not like what I saw. "I can't even please myself. How can I please anyone else, especially my Maker?"

"What a miserable creature I am! Who will rescue me from this body bound for death? Thanks be to G-d, he will!--through Yeshua the Messiah, our Lord!" (Romans 6:24, 25.)

I am N. Y. Twinh. My name is <u>Not</u> <u>Y</u>eshua (Jesus), <u>That's</u> <u>Why</u> <u>I</u> <u>Need</u> <u>Him</u>!

I HAVE BLOOD ON MY HANDS!

"Oh, G-d! Thousands of my brethren have fallen to the ground. Their bodies have been ripped apart and cast into the street. A great evil has been done in my land. People who defy your name have done this atrocity. They have attacked all that we hold sacred and have killed our people. Oh, G-d! Arise and come to our aid. Oh, G-d! Bless us and expand our territory. Allow not our enemies to triumph over us. Oh, G-d! We come to you in prayer and hold a day of remembrance for our brethren and beseech you to take vengeance on our foes. Oh, G-d! The blood of our brethren cries to you and we call upon you to rid this evil from the face of the earth."

"Who is this that approaches me with blood on his hands?" responds the Lord of Hosts.

"It is I your humble servant. I beseech you Lord. Avenge this blood of my fallen brethren. Grant me victory over my evil enemies who have committed this murderous act of terror."

"Avenge the blood of your brethren, I will most certainly do! But, first, I must avenge the blood that cries to me from your hands, the blood of the millions you have slaughtered in the name of your god, FREEDOM," says the Lord of Hosts.

"Woe is me! Woe is me! I am America, and I have blood on my hands!"

"You can't serve ADONAI; because he is a holy G-d, a jealous G-d, and he will not forgive your crimes and sins. If you abandon ADONAI and serve foreign gods, he will turn, doing you harm and destroying you after he has done you good." (Y'hoshua/Joshua 24:19)

"Who is this that approaches me in the name of so many gods? Who is this that seeks my blessing while invoking the names of other gods that are not gods? Are you so full of pride that you dare to approach The King of Kings in a manner I have not prescribed? Have you forgotten that if it were not for my grace, my Holiness would strike you down?

"Woe to you who calls good evil, and evil good. You say you are good and that you will "wipe out evil"? By what standard do you judge yourself? How did you obtain such goodness and become appointed the avenger upon the wicked?

"Since you have cast my Law to the ground, and have replaced it with one of your own making; since you cast it to the ground and forbid your children from learning from it in their schools; since you rewrite it so that it does not offend you or hurt your feelings; since you have determined that it is full of hate and unworthy to be hung on your walls; let me remind you of the Torah I gave you through my servant, Moshe.

ALEPH - "I am ADONAI your G-d, who brought Israel out of the land of Egypt, out of the abode of slavery.

BET - "You shall have no other gods before me. You are not to make for yourselves a carved image or any kind of representation of anything in heaven above, or the earth beneath or in the water below the shoreline. You are not to bow down to them or serve them; for I, ADONAI your G-d, am a jealous G-d, punishing the children for the sins of the parents to the third and fourth generation of those who hate me, but displaying grace to the thousandth generation of those who love me and obey my mitzvot.

GIMMEL - "You are not to use lightly the name of ADONAI your G-d, because ADONAI will not leave unpunished someone who uses his name lightly.

"Why then do you hold hands with idolaters and invoke the names of their gods when you pray to me? Are their gods equal to me? Did I not proclaim through my servant, Moshe, that you are not to invoke the names of other gods or even let them be heard crossing your lips? If their gods are so important to you and you see them as equal to me, then why do you not pray to them? You protect and "respect" them and call them your own. Then pray to them and ask them to save you. If they are so mighty, then what do you need me for?

"My name is not 'God,' as in 'G-O-D,' the generic 'God.' My name is YHVH, ADONAI-Tzva'ot, and my Son's name is

Yeshua your Messiah. Why then do you approach me in the name of gods that are not gods? I am ADONAI, the True and Living G-D. YESHUA is my Son, and Moshe is one of my many prophets.

"Did I not tell you that Yeshua is my Son, in whom I am well pleased? Is it not his blood that was shed for your sins? Why then do you approach me in the name of dead people, Allah, the "Virgin," Saint So-&-So, or any other name that is not my Son's? Did I not tell you that none can come to the Father except through the Son? Why then do you mix His blood with the blood of others? He is my chosen one. He is the Pesach Lamb of G-d, and by no other name shall you seek my face! There is no other who has redeemed you! There is no other who mediates for you! No other has atoned for your sins! The Son of David is the only one who is worthy to approach me as your advocate! How dare you defile my name! How dare you desecrate the Blood of my Son!

DALET - "Remember the day, Shabbat, to set it apart for G-d. You have six days to labor and do all your work, but the seventh day is a Shabbat for ADONAI your G-d. On it, you are not to do any kind of work -- not you, your son or your daughter, not your male or female slave, not your livestock, and not the foreigner staying with you inside the gates to your property. For in six days, ADONAI made heaven and earth, the sea and everything in them; but on the seventh day he rested. This is why ADONAI blessed the day, Shabbat, and separated it for himself.

"Who commanded you to change my commandments? Not that you keep them anyway. But, tell me, by what authority did you take it upon yourself to change that which I wrote with my own finger into the stone tablets I handed my servant, Moshe? Did I not say that until heaven and earth pass away, not so much as a yud or a stroke will pass from the Torah; not until everything that must happen has happened? Jump up and down! Stomp your feet! Is the earth still underneath you? Then, how dare you change my words!

"I tell you again, Yesha'yahu was right when he prophesied about you hypocrites--as it is written, "These people honor me with their lips, but their hearts are far away from me. Their worship of me is useless, because they teach man-made rules as if they were doctrines." You depart from G-d's commandment and hold onto human tradition. Indeed, you have made a fine art of departing from G-d's command in order to keep your tradition!

"Do I take as much pleasure in burnt offerings and sacrifices as in obeying what I say? What is Lent to me? Why do you still weep for Tammuz? Does it please me that you make petty sacrifices to me while you profane MY Sabbath and my commandments? Surely obeying is better than sacrifice, and heeding orders than the fat of rams. For rebellion is like the sin of sorcery, stubbornness like the crime of idolatry.

"So some of you do not forsake gathering together to worship me on various days of the week. Continue to meet and worship, but do not proclaim that which I did not! Did I or did I not proclaim the seventh day to be the Shabbat? Then, do likewise, and proclaim it as such!

HEY - "Honor your father and mother, so that you may live long in the land which ADONAI your G-d is giving you.

"Why are you so amazed that your children hate you and despise you? Why do they despair and seek their own destruction or the destruction of those around them? Because you do not honor your Father which is in heaven. Nor do you teach them my commandments as I instructed you to do in the beginning. Like father, like son. You have begotten your own kind; they are like you, rebellious and fearless. You do not fear me. Why then, are you so surprised that they are so fearless, rebellious, and full of rage?

VAV - "Do not murder.

"The Blood of your Messiah was shed for you so that your sin would be forgiven and so that you would be free from the power of sin. There is no need for you to shed blood to enter my Paradise. Messiah's blood is Holy and Pure. His Blood is your Atonement! If you call upon His name and ask for my grace, I will surely hear you and redeem you.

"Yet, you mistakenly use your "freedom" to pursue that which you see right in your own eyes. In the name of your freedom, you murder my children. You sacrifice your children to Molech; that detestable act which never entered my mind. You experiment with their bodies to make yourself wise, only to bring

6

judgment on your own head. Your hands are covered in blood! You wage war to protect those who bow to the moon, when it's "in your national interest." Yet, you turn your face from your own brethren as they are slaughtered by those who bow to the moon, all for the sake of "your national interest." You have blood on your hands!

ZAYIN - "Do not commit adultery.

"Not only do you spread your legs and prostitute yourself to the lowest bidder, but you exchange the natural for the unnatural and, in my own name, you call it holy and good. Woe to you who call evil good and good evil, who change darkness into light and light into darkness, who change bitter into sweet and sweet into bitter! The phrase, 'living in sin' is no longer heard among you. Taking another's spouse is no longer strange to you. Divorce is even rampant among those who call themselves my children. How far your hearts have drifted away from me!

CHET - "Do not steal.

"You take advantage of my widows and orphans. You steal from the poor and give to the rich. You take bribes under the table, while you smile and kiss the babies. You raise your children to live off of the efforts of your neighbors and expect your neighbor to work for your sustenance. You rob me of my tithes and offerings to build your own little kingdom. You do this and more while coming to me with praise on your lips.

TET - "Do not give false evidence against your neighbor.

"Anything to get ahead in life, so you tell yourself. Do I not see? Do I not hear? Do you forget that I will hold you accountable for all your deeds and thoughts? I see what you do and hear what you say in secret and I know all your plots. Vengeance is mine and I will repay.

YOD - "Do not covet your neighbor's house; do not covet your neighbor's wife, his male or his female slave, his ox, his donkey or anything that belongs to your neighbor.

"You are not content with what you have. Your cistern is not good enough for you. Your lust for that which is not yours consumes you like a dog in heat. When you obtain that which is not yours, you are not content, but seek out another. Your belly is your god and your genitals are your guide.

"Why should I forgive you? Your people have abandoned me and sworn by non-gods. When I fed them to the full, they committed adultery, thronging to the brothels. They have become like well-fed horses, lusty stallions, each one neighing after his neighbor's wife. Should I not punish for this? Should I not be avenged on a nation like this?"

"Wisdom calls aloud in the open air and raises her voice in the public places; she calls out at street corners and speaks out at entrances to city gates: 'How long, you whose lives have no purpose, will you love thoughtless living? How long will scorners find pleasure in mocking? How long will fools hate knowledge? Repent when I reprove -- I will pour out my spirit to you, I will make my words known to you. Because you refused when I called, and no one paid attention when I put out my hand, but instead you neglected my counsel and would not accept my reproof; I, in turn, will laugh at your distress, and mock when terror comes over you-- yes, when terror overtakes you like a storm and your disaster approaches like a whirlwind, when distress and trouble assail you, Then they will call me, but I won't answer; they will seek me earnestly, but they won't find me. Because they hated knowledge and did not choose the fear of ADONAI, they refused my counsel and despised my reproof. So they will bear the consequences of their own way and be overfilled with their own schemes. For the aimless wandering of the thoughtless will kill them, and the smug overconfidence of fools will destroy them; but those who pay attention to me will live securely, untroubled by fear of misfortune.'" (Mishlei/Proverbs 1:20-33)

"ADONAI'S arm is not too short to save, nor is his ear too dull to hear. Rather, it is your own crimes that separate you from your G-d; your sins have hidden his face from you, so that he doesn't hear. ***FOR YOUR HANDS ARE STAINED WITH BLOOD*** *and your fingers with crime; your lips speak lies, your tongues utter wicked things....Their feet run to evil, they rush to shed innocent blood, their thoughts are thoughts of wickedness, their paths lead to havoc and ruin. The way of shalom they do not know, their goings-about obey no law, they make devious paths*

8

for themselves; no one treading them will ever know shalom."
(Yesha'yahu/Isaiah 59:1-8)

YOU ARE N.Y. TWYNH

Former Minnesota Governor, Jesse, "the former body and then the mind," Ventura, made a statement shortly after his election to office about organized religion being for the "weak-minded." What did you think of that?

Many in organized religion took great offense at his words. But is he right or wrong? Is there any truth to what he said? Or is he just a narrow minded anti-religion person?

I'm not going to take pot-shots at the man. For that is what he is, a man. I haven't heard him claim to be perfect or better than anyone else. Far from it. I believe he has bragged about his imperfections and stated that's what got him elected. People in Minnesota wanted someone they could relate to better, and chose him as their Governor. So be it.

However, let's not cast his words aside. I'm not going to attempt to explain his words for him. He's a big man, real big. He can defend himself.

But, is religion for the strong or the weak? Who claims to be perfect in this world of ours? Let him or her stand now and proclaim their perfection!

That's what I thought. I don't know anyone who claims perfection. Do you?

Yet, countless people will say they are "good."

"I'm not a murderer/rapist/prostitute/Hitler/etc." "I treat others with respect and believe that everyone has a right to their own way of seeing things." "I'm not going to hell." "I'm a good person." "I go to church/synagogue/temple, sometimes/all the time/once in a while." "I don't need church. I get with my higher power on my own time."

I wasn't raised in church. I first attended church on a regular basis when I was 13. My brothers and I all went and got baptized in order of our birth, at different times that year. It was quite awesome. Our parents didn't go until a few years later. Back then, we attended a Southern Baptist Church, which I am proud and unashamed to admit, in spite of what you will read in this book.

Today, I'm the only one who stuck with it. I asked my second brother why he stopped going to church. He told me that he liked to party and drink with his buddies. He liked to go dancing on Saturday nights and "have a good time."

He said to me, "I stopped going to church because I felt like a hypocrite. Church taught that I couldn't drink and dance. I like to drink and dance. But, I couldn't go out and party on Saturday nights and then go to church on Sunday like others would. I didn't want to be a hypocrite. So, I chose to party." At least he was honest. Are we as honest ourselves?

I pray my family and friends will come to know the love of G-d and put their trust in Yeshua as their Messiah. Their past experiences and the things that they were taught seem to have blinded many like them. Maybe you are like them. I hope this book will break down some of those "false" walls that keep you from entering G-d's Kingdom. I hope you will look to G-d and His Word, both written and living, as your guide for your life, rather than to men and their doctrines and traditions.

I was the Bible trivia champion in church. The kids raised in church didn't really like me that much because I took G-d too seriously. Like most, I loved church camp too.

As I mentioned, I was raised a "good heathen." I *said* the "sinner's prayer" when I was 13 and got baptized. But, you know, I don't think I fully understood what "born again" really was until I was 17.

The summer between my junior and senior years in high school, I was working for one of my dad's friends making boat docks at White River Lake in Texas. I'm not sure what he thought of me. I would take my pocket New Testament with Psalms and Proverbs with me and read it during lunch. Something wasn't right. I wasn't content within myself.

During that summer, I had a soul searching experience that I will keep short here. I attended a "tent meeting" out of curiosity. It was my first. I didn't like what I heard. I didn't like the bucket being brought out for donations at the end either. It was a big bucket too. "Come and bring your offerings and receive a miracle." No miracles happened that night.

I don't recall Yeshua (Jesus) ever asking for an offering in exchange for touching peoples' lives, do you? Can you see Yeshua handing out bottles of "stuff" in exchange for "seed money" so that He can pray for them to receive their miracle from the Father? I can't. (I will use Yeshua's Hebrew name, as his Hebrew mother called him. You will understand why as you read along.)

I know Paul passed out pieces of cloth that he prayed over, but I don't recall him getting "seed money" in exchange for them. I'm not opposed to "seed money" being given to a ministry. G-d will bless a cheerful giver. Generosity is looked on well by G-d. But the teaching of giving in exchange for a miracle borders on spiritual quackery. Anyway...

I didn't have a Bible with me and was asking someone to lend me one. After the meeting, while searching the scriptures for something, a man in his 30's and a boy about 12 approached me.

Come to find out, according to them, Yeshua didn't rise from the dead like He said he would. "No, his body turned to dust," the man said.

"Dust!?" I couldn't believe my ears. I had to find it. Where was it? I couldn't find it. Maybe I was wrong. Maybe they were right. After all, who am I to argue? I was only 17 and not raised in church.

I went home frustrated and shaken. My family had gone out of town for the weekend. I was working at the lake during the week and came home for the weekend. I had the house to myself. We didn't have central heating and air then. We just had a window unit in my parents' room. So, I was staying in there while they were gone. As I sat on my parents' bed, I searched G-d's word like a treasure hunter digging for treasure.

"I know it's in there. Where is it?...Ah! Here it is..."

"Why are you so upset? Why are these doubts welling up inside you? Look at my hands and my feet -- it is I, myself! Touch me and see -- a ghost doesn't have flesh and bones, as you see I do." (Luke 24:38, 39.)

"There it is! I knew it was there somewhere," I proclaimed with excitement. But notice. Those to whom He spoke these words still wondered if it was so...

"As he said this, he showed them his hands and feet. While they were still unable to believe it for joy and stood there dumbfounded, he said to them, Have you something here to eat?

"They gave him a piece of broiled fish, which he took it and ate in their presence. (Still believe Yeshua was a vegetarian?)

"Yeshua said to them, 'This is what I meant when I was still with you and told you that everything written about me in the Torah of Moshe, the Prophets and the Psalms had to be fulfilled.'" (Do you believe the Old Covenant writings are not for us?)

"Then he opened their minds, so that they could understand the Tanakh, telling them, 'Here is what it says: the Messiah is to suffer and to rise from the dead on the third day; and in his name repentance leading to forgiveness of sins is to be proclaimed to people of all nations, starting with Yerushalayim." (Luke 24:40-47)

For four years I attended church calling myself a Christian. That night, I truly believed in faith and had my true born again experience, and became a true believer in the Messiah of mankind.

A few years ago, my wife and I spent eight months in South Korea teaching conversational English to professionals and university students. I had a conversation with a Buddhist one night. I asked him to tell me about Buddha. He told me that Buddha was a man that became god. I asked if he believes in hell. He said he did. I asked if Buddha made hell. He said yes. I asked him if he didn't want to go to hell. He said no, he doesn't want to go to hell.

"Well then," I asked, "if Buddha was a man like you and I, and he became a god who made hell, why then don't you become a god and destroy hell and send everyone to heaven?"

Speechless. His face showed his bewilderment at my question. I don't know what came of him, but I am sure he thought good and hard after that night. Oh yes, I know there is more to Buddhism than this, but this was the actual conversation we had. The bottom line is that Buddha can't save you. Yeshua, the Messiah, can and will if you ask him to.

Maybe you believe in Buddha, or in Rama and Shiva. Maybe you believe in your own made up theology or philosophy about life, or some other god who is not a god. Maybe you believe in Muhammed's religion, which he started on his own (taken from the Torah of the Jews and built on the reputation of Jesus) that has produced the "fruit" of death and destruction from the slaughter of millions over the centuries, Christians, Jews, and even Muslims.

By the way, it sure is ironic that in Saudi Arabia, the home of Mecca, is a mountain on the northwest side called Jabal al Lawz. The locals call it the Mt. of Moses. Yes, <u>the real Mt. Sinai is in Saudi Arabia</u>, the "land of Midyan." Ask Bob Cornuke about it. He's been there.

You can thank G. Gordon Liddy for enlightening me to that fact. A friend of mine was listening to his show back in 1997 or 98 when I happened to come in the room and hear Mr. Liddy talking to Howard Blum, author of the book, "The Gold of Exodus." It is about the adventures of Larry Williams and Bob Cornuke as they searched for the real Mt. Sinai with G-d's word as their guide. Unless these guys are a couple of con-artists, it would be nice to let the world see the proof and verify if what they saw is still there.

If our "friends," the Saudis, would be open enough to let us see, maybe we could all take a look at the mountain with the burnt top, burned by G-d's fiery furnace, along with all the other archeological discoveries Bob Cornuke, and his associates found. This would settle the issue once and for all regarding Jerusalem and the land and people of Israel.

No, don't count on it. For the keepers of Islam to reveal to the world evidence of Moses and the G-d of Israel, would undermine everything Islam claims to be true. Like most powerful leaders of nations and religious organizations, they prefer to keep their people in ignorance and dictate what their membership is to believe, even when the truth stares them in the face. How much does the common peace loving man and woman of any religion or nation truly know about that which their leadership claims to know? "We are all like sheep who have gone astray."

One more side note about Muhammed that he should be admired for and that puts the "Christian West" to shame. I've heard it said that Muhammed stole the Persian War god, named Allah and did away with the rest of the 359 Persian gods. I found this to be inaccurate according to a former Shiite Muslim who discovered the truth about Yeshua and now calls upon the Messiah for his salvation.

Pay attention "Christian"! For you who say you believe in the Ten Commandments, this puts you to shame when you defend the destruction of giant Buddhas and other "cultural artifacts." I do not at all propose you or anyone go and destroy someone else's idols. But why are you so quick to defend the idols of others while you cast G-d's commandments to the ground, disregarding them and despising them?

The "real" story goes something like this: Muhammed destroyed all the idols of the religious community except for the one god whose name pronounced similar to Allah. When the leaders of the community arrived in the morning to see only this one idol standing, they asked Muhammed why he had destroyed all the gods.

Muhammed responded saying that he didn't do it, "that god over there did it," as he pointed to the idol of the war/moon god. They were shocked and upset. They responded to Muhammed that "that god couldn't have destroyed the others because it is only stone." "Then why do you worship idols," he replied.

Thus, began his movement to cleanse the land of idolatry and calling them back to worship of the Creator in Heaven. Muhammed is to be praised for his stand against the idolatry of the people. Or was this story about Abraham and not Muhammed? I have heard this story with credit given to Abraham as well.

If you say with your lips that idolatry is an abomination and offense unto the Living G-d, then why do you defend idolatry in the name of "cultural diversity" or "historical preservation"?

Muhammed's example, or Abraham's, in this case, puts us to shame. His teachings of ONE G-d are true and many of the teachings of the Koran are to be respected, especially those which come from Moses and Jesus. However, where the Koran diverts, is where we are to also divert and cease to listen to it.

Yes, Islam accepts Moses and Jesus as prophets, but does not accept Jesus as the Son of G-d, and as Emmanuel, G-d With Us.

"Dear friends, don't trust every spirit. On the contrary, test the spirits to see whether they are from G-d; because many false prophets have gone out into the world. Here is how you recognize the Spirit of G-d: every spirit which acknowledges that Yeshua the Messiah came as a human being is from G-d, and every spirit which does not acknowledge Yeshua is not from G-d -- in fact, this is the spirit of the Anti-Messiah." (1 Yochanan/John 4:1-3)

Yes, Islam acknowledges Yeshua as a man. BUT, not as G-d!

"In the beginning was the Word, and the Word was with G-d, and the WORD WAS G-D. He was with G-d in the beginning. All things came to be through him, and without him nothing made had being. In him was life, and the life was the light of mankind. The light shines in the darkness, and the darkness has not suppressed it.... This was the true light, which gives light to everyone entering the world. He was in the world -- the world came to be through him -- yet the world did not know him. He came to his own homeland, yet his own people did not receive him. But to as many as did receive him, to those who put their trust in his person and power, he gave the right to become children of G-d, not because of bloodline, physical impulse or human intention, but because of G-d. THE WORD BECAME A HUMAN BEING and lived with us, and we saw his Sh'khinah, The Sh'khinah of the Father's only Son, full of grace and truth....We have all received from his fullness, yes, grace upon grace. For the Torah was given through Moshe; grace and truth came through Yeshua the Messiah." (Yochanan/John 1:1-17)

"I am astounded that you are so quick to remove yourselves from me, the one who called you by the Messiah's grace, and turn to some other supposedly "Good News," which is not good news at all! What is really happening is that certain people are pestering you and trying to pervert the genuine Good News of the Messiah. But even if we -- or, for that matter, an ANGEL FROM HEAVEN! -- were to announce to you some so-called "Good

News" contrary to the Good News we did announce to you, let him be under a curse forever! We said it before, and I say it again: if anyone announces "Good News" contrary to what you received, let him be under a curse forever!" (Galatians 1:6-9)

THIS is the gulf that separates Islam and reveals it as another Satanic lie. There is no need to study and understand Islam America! To understand the Muslim is one thing. To study Islam and teach it to your children is another. This is all you need to know. It is a lie! Islam was started by a man who was a murderer and an adulterer. He started out with good intentions, but was led astray by a deceptive spirit, claiming to be the angel Gabriel. (See the above scripture again.) Muhammed had many wives and spent his life murdering and pillaging the peaceful people of Arabia, Africa, Europe, and Asia. His fruits bear him out. According to Yeshua, the righteous one, the spirit of Islam is opposed to the truth and love of the G-d of Grace. Ask the Messiah! His is the perfect one! Muhammed is not!

Even the Koran speaks of the Messiah Yeshua being the only righteous and sinless man who ever lived. I say nothing different than what the Koran tells us. Except that The Word of G-d, who is the Light of the World, IS G-D HIMSELF WHO BECAME A MAN AND LIVED AMONG US. This same Yeshua is the one Muhammed and the Koran call merely a man. Who will you believe? Muhammed or Messiah Yeshua?

The Koran teaches that Yeshua was a "created man" and was taken up to be with Allah until the Day of Judgment. At the Day of Judgment, this "man" shall return and destroy the infidels.

Yeshua was certainly a man, and he will most certainly return to judge and destroy the wicked. But, contrary to the teachings of Islam, this same Yeshua said himself that he came not to destroy the wicked, but to save the wicked from their sins. Jihad is not of Yeshua!

Yeshua teaches salvation by grace through faith and trust in Him. Muhammed and his followers teach "submission," or death to those who resist. Even if one submits to Islam, one is not guaranteed Paradise. Islam is a religion of fear and death. Even though a Muslim's good outweighs his/her bad, he/she still is not assured a place, unless they die while killing non-Muslims for the cause of Allah. This is why they strive to keep their laws, which according to Muhammed, have their origin in the Torah of YHVH given through Moses. For clarification, killing to get into Paradise does not come from Torah.

Sure Muslim people are peace loving people. What Muslim mother does not love her children? What Muslim father does not take pride in his son? What Muslim family does not weep at the death of a loved one, or rejoice at the wedding of a daughter? What Muslim man or woman does not desire peace and tranquility and a place of their own to call home?

Likewise, what non-Muslim person does not desire the same? Having lived in an Asian land, I can attest to you that the desire for peace and love are universal. Western nations are not alone in the "civilized" aspirations for peace and love. It is the desire of every human heart.

Islam regards Moshe as a prophet and the Torah as from G-d. Then let us consult the words of Moshe in G-d's Torah:

"When you enter the land ADONAI your G-d is giving you, you are not to learn how to follow the abominable practices of those nations. There must not be found among you anyone who makes his son or daughter pass through fire, a diviner, a soothsayer, an enchanter, a sorcerer, a spell-caster, a consulter of ghosts or spirits, or a necromancer...

"For whoever does these things is detestable to ADONAI, and because of these abominations ADONAI your G-d is driving them out ahead of you. You must be wholehearted with ADONAI your G-d. For these nations, which you are about to dispossess, listen to soothsayers and diviners; but you, ADONAI your G-d does not allow you to do this.

"ADONAI will raise up for you a prophet like me from among yourselves, from your own kinsmen. You are to pay attention to him, just as when you were assembled at Horev and requested ADONAI your G-d, 'Don't let me hear the voice of ADONAI my G-d any more, or let me see this great fire ever again; if I do, I will die!' On that occasion ADONAI said to me, 'They are right in what they are saying.

"I will raise up for them a prophet like you from among their kinsmen. I will put my words in his mouth, and he will tell them

everything I order him. Whoever doesn't listen to my words, which he will speak in my name, will have to account for himself to me." (D'varim/Deuteronomy 18:9-19)

This prophet Moshe speaks of is a "Jew" from the lineage of Israel. Yeshua was/is a Jew. Muhammed is not. Listen to Yeshua, not Muhammed. Yeshua is the Prophet of G-d, to whom we are to pay our attention, to listen to, and obey.

Let's not forget that Muhammed did not 'start' his religion until 630 A.C.E., almost 600 years after Titus destroyed the Jewish Temple in Jerusalem, which the Palestinians like to deny ever existed. But that's a story straight out of Bible history and prophecy that is now playing before our very eyes.

"A prophecy, the word of ADONAI concerning Isra'el -- here is the message from ADONAI, who stretched out the heavens, laid the foundation of the earth and formed the spirit inside human beings:

"I will make Yerushalayim a cup that will stagger the surrounding peoples. Even Y'hudah will be caught up in the siege against Yerushalayim. When that day comes, I will make Yerushalayim a heavy stone for all the peoples. All who try to lift it will hurt themselves, and all the earth's nations will be massed against her.

"When that day comes,' says ADONAI, 'I will strike all the horses with panic and their riders with madness; I will keep watch over Y'hudah, but I will strike blind all the horses of the peoples.

"The leaders of Y'hudah will say to themselves, 'Those living in Yerushalayim are my strength through ADONAI-Tzva'ot their G-d.'

"When that day comes, I will make the leaders of Y'hudah like a blazing fire pan in a pile of wood, like a fiery torch among sheaves of grain; they will devour all the surrounding peoples, on the right and on the left. Yerushalayim will be inhabited in her own place, Yerushalayim.

"ADONAI will save the tents of Y'hudah first, so that the glory of the house of David and the glory of those living in Yerushalayim will not appear greater than that of Y'hudah.

"When that day comes, I will seek to destroy all nations attacking Yerushalayim; and I will pour out on the house of David and on those living in Yerushalayim a spirit of grace and prayer; and they will look to me, whom they pierced.

"They will mourn for him as one mourns for an only son; they will be in bitterness on his behalf like the bitterness for a firstborn son. When that day comes, there will be great mourning in Yerushalayim, mourning like that for Hadad-Rimmon in the Megiddo Valley." (Z'kharyah/Zechariah 12:1-11)

Believe what you want, but I choose to believe in the G-d who became a man and whose grave is empty and whose name causes demons to tremble and men to shiver with terrorizing anxiety. I choose to put my faith in the one who is called **Wonderful, Counselor, <u>Mighty G-d</u>, Everlasting Father, Prince of Peace; and whose name means Salvation, Yeshua ha Mashiach, <u>Yeshua the Messiah</u>, aka, Jesus the Christ.**

Did you know that Yeshua is Hebrew for Salvation? "And his name shall be Salvation, for he shall save his people." Puts it in a clearer light, doesn't it? (In this book, I purposely use some Hebrew pronunciations for the purpose of clarification and to challenge your thinking.)

For those of you who dare to equate Islam with the faith of Abraham and his Seed, let me remind you of the words spoken to the human woman named Miryam (Mary):

"Look! You will become pregnant, you will give birth to a son, and you are to name him Yeshua. He will be great, he will be called <u>Son of Ha'Elyon</u>. ADONAI, G-d, will give him the throne of his forefather David; and he will rule the House of Ya'akov (Israel) forever -- there will be no end to his Kingdom...The Ruach HaKodesh will come over you, the power of Ha'Elyon will cover you. Therefore the holy child born to you will be called the <u>Son of G-d</u>." (Luke 1: 31-35)

G-D has a Son! G-D'S name is YHVH and His Son's name is YESHUA!

I use YHVH to emphasize that this G-d is not a generic G-d to be confused with any other god, like Allah, or any other name. His name is YHVH and he is to be treated in the way he commands. The Y is for the Hebrew letter "yod," the H is for "hey," the V is for "vav," and the H is for "hey" again.

ADONAI is a title used to replace the YHVH in the Bible version I quote in this book. I use YHVH in my book to distinguish for the reader that YHVH is not a generic god who is to be taken lightly or compared to any other. Be careful and treat His Name Holy, as it is!

I know that shortly after the World Trade Center's tragic destruction, many started to pray to "God" and were impressed by the "unity" of people praying to "God." But do not be deceived! The Holy One of Abraham, Isaac, and Israel will not be mocked and he will not share his throne with any other. He is not impressed like men are. President George W. Bush did not speak for G-d on this particular matter! Franklin Graham was right when he spoke out on this. He had no reason to apologize!

Looking back to that summer of my searching for G-d's saving truth, I think I can relate to the man who was a teacher in Israel during the time of Yeshua. I had already read the whole Bible a few times and knew more than most of those who were raised in church. I had knowledge of good and evil and was devoted to my Bible studies and attended church as often as the church doors were open.

What was his name? I think it was Nakdimon (Hebrew), Nicodemus (English). Yes, Nicodemus was his name. It's in that section where the scripture that so many people like to quote is located. That verse would be John 3:16. I'm sure you've see it on televised sporting events, usually behind home plate or the football goal.

Interesting. You hear everyone quote John 3:16. Many homosexual "Christians" like to make that their battle cry. Many "Christians" like to make that their battle cry. Many non-Christians like to quote it when they feel pressured to see that their "goodness" is not good enough along with that most often misquoted verse about "not judging."

So many people want G-d's forgiveness. So many people want eternal life. So many people want to be accepted by G-d. So many people want the blessings without paying the price. It's like freedom in America. Everyone wants it, but not everyone is willing to fight for it. The current "War against Terrorism" appears to be revealing how true that is.

Have you heard the following? And if so, how often have you heard it?

"For G-d so loved the world that he gave his only and unique Son, so that everyone who trusts in him may have everlasting life, instead of being utterly destroyed. For G-d did not send the Son into the world to judge the world, but rather so that through him, the world might be saved. Those who trust in him are not judged: (Yochanan/John 3:16-17)

As proclaimed by all our Muslim neighbors, Islam claims that "Allah has no son." This clearly contradicts Messianic Judaism, more commonly known as Christianity. Contrary to the proclamations of President Barack Obama in 2009, the two religions are NOT similar, they are contradictory. For as the Jewish prophets proclaimed throughout their writings, particularly Yesha'yahu, aka Isaiah, YHVH's son would suffer and take the punishment meant for you and me upon himself. Yesha'yahu/Isaiah 53! Why is it not read in the synagogues? The same reason it is not read in the mosques. It proclaims the truth of G-d's Son being the Atonement for mankind.

"Who believes our report? To whom is the arm of ADONAI revealed? For before him he grew up like a young plant, like a root out of dry ground. He was not well-formed or especially handsome; we saw him, but his appearance did not attract us. People despised and avoided him, a man of pains, well acquainted with illness. Like someone from whom people turn their faces, he was despised; we did not value him.

"In fact, it was our diseases he bore, our pains from which he suffered; yet we regarded him as punished, stricken and afflicted by G-d. But he was wounded because of our crimes, crushed because of our sins; the disciplining that makes us whole fell on him, and by his bruises we are healed.

"We all, like sheep, went astray; we turned, each one, to his own way; yet ADONAI laid on him the guilt of all of us.

"Though mistreated, he was submissive -- he did not open his mouth. Like a lamb led to be slaughtered, like a sheep silent before its shearers, he did not open his mouth. After forcible

arrest and sentencing, he was taken away; and none of his generation protested his being cut off from the land of the living for the crimes of my people, who deserved the punishment themselves....

Messiah Yeshua did not make the nations "submit" to him by conquering with the sword. He submitted himself as the Pesach Lamb of G-d and gave himself as the sacrifice for all mankind's sins. **Men have misrepresented him and his teachings** as they used the sword to conquer through the Crusades and Inquisitions.

The spirit of Islamic pogroms is no different than the spirit of "Christian" pogroms. They both are inspired by Satan and not by G-d. Do not call murder and forced confession "Christian" just because those who committed or commit such crimes call themselves "Christians." G-d will judge and destroy the wicked, but not through the hands of true Christians!

"He was given a grave among the wicked; in his death he was with a rich man. Although he had done no violence and had said nothing deceptive, yet it pleased ADONAI to crush him with illness, to see if he would present himself as a guilt offering. If he does, he will see his offspring; and he will prolong his days; and at his hand ADONAI'S desire will be accomplished.

"After this ordeal, he will see satisfaction. 'By his knowing [pain and sacrifice], my righteous servant makes many righteous; it is for their sins that he suffers....

"Therefore I will assign him a share with the great, he will divide the spoil with the mighty, for having exposed himself to death and being counted among the sinners, while actually bearing the sin of many and interceding for the offenders." (Yesha'yahu/Isaiah 53)

No need for flagellation! Stop whipping yourselves and making yourselves bleed. Messiah has bled for your sins. Stop the penance! Turn to G-d and call on Messiah to save you from your sins.

But, don't stop there. Continue the words of John...

"those who do not trust have been judged already, in that they have not trusted in the one who is G-d's only and unique Son. Now this is the judgment: the light has come into the world,

but people loved the darkness rather than the light. Why? Because their actions were wicked.

"For everyone who does evil things hates the light and avoids it, so that his actions won't be exposed. But everyone who does what is true comes to the light, so that all may see his actions are accomplished through G-d." (Yochanan/John 3:18-21.)

Did you see the movie, "A Few Good Men," with Jack Nicholson and Tom Cruise? Do you remember the famous words when Tom Cruise's character vehemently demands the truth?

"You can't handle the truth!!!!!" yells the Colonel.

Can you handle the truth? Many in this world can't.

It amazes me at times. I come across some every now and then. Some believe in G-d, but don't believe that G-d will accept them into heaven. Amazing. There are many people out there who can't believe the words of Yeshua, the Messiah. "I'm going to hell and there's nothing I can do about it," they proclaims *in faith*. What can you do for people like that, but pray? Many can't accept John 3:17-21. Yet, many others can't accept John 3:16. Why is that?

Which one are you? Do you call yourself a Believer, yet struggle with these yourself? Do you take the part you can swallow and hope the rest isn't true? Have you found Yeshua (Salvation) yet? Jesse, "the body and mind," Ventura...What about your spirit? Well, it's dead like everyone else's! Yours too, Oprah!

"All have sinned and come short of earning G-d's praise." (Romans 3:23)

Why not admit the truth dear reader...**You are N. Y. TWYNH. You are <u>N</u>ot <u>Y</u>eshua, <u>T</u>hat's <u>W</u>hy <u>Y</u>OU <u>N</u>eed <u>H</u>im!**

OUCH!

"Ouch! @#%*&!"

Have you ever hit your thumb with a hammer while trying to hit the nail, or slam it in a door? When you did, didn't you hold your hand tightly to your chest and squeeze your eyes tightly shut as you focused on your throbbing hurt.

Although some of us rant and rave, and some spout vulgarities, most all of us will still grab our thumb with our other hand and bring it close to try to make the pain stop. This is natural! It is our body's way of protecting and comforting itself.

"Ouch!!!" we shout at first. Then we grab our pain and pull it close.

"Owwwwwooooo!..." we start to moan as the initial pain transforms into a throbbing ache.

"Mmmmmmmffh," we quiet the expression of our pain down to an inner concentration on the hurting member of our body, hoping to make it better by our force of will.

Yet, no matter how much we focus on it, time seems to be the only remedy in the healing process.

Add to this throbbing ache an open wound. Not only did you hit your thumb, but you made it bleed as well. Now, we have more than just an ache. We also have a wound that needs tending to. The throb will subside with time, but the open wound will become infected if not dealt with properly.

And we all know what that would lead to. Yes, of course, difficulty in tying our shoes.

"But it hurts!" we yell to our dad as we turn away from his reach.

"Let me see. It's bleeding," he proclaims with great concern.

"Aaaagh!" we cry as we clinch it close to our chest, hoping that the pain will go away.

"If you don't let me tend to it, it will only get worse," explains dad.

As we whimper to ourselves in agony, clinching the bloody soar, we can't help but think in our minds, and sometimes scream out loud, "Leave me alone! I'll be all right!" Just don't think about it, we tell ourselves. Ignore it and it will go away, so we hope.

Likewise, we go through life holding our hearts so tightly that we close our eyes to the world around us as we focus on our hurts. Our pain is real and very personal. We do not want it exposed to the elements. We want it to stop! We want it to feel better, don't we?

My father was the youngest of ten children. He passed away September 11, 2008 after a long fight with cancer. God rest his soul. I remember the pain on his face as my mother and I sat with him a few days before he died. However, the pain I saw wasn't from the physical pain, it was from the mental anguish from whatever memories he was dealing with in his soul. I thank God for the opportunity to spend time with him and exchange some heartfelt words with him before his passing.

G-d said "the wages of sin is death."

Sin is more serious than a thumb smashing and more deadly than any disease. Sin kills both body and spirit!

I originally wrote most of this book a year and a half before the September 11th terrorist attack on the World Trade Center in New York. With the pain of that event, look at how our nation dealt with it and is still dealing with it. For the most part, the nation took time to "dress the wound." Yet there are many, far too many, that have not tended to the wound properly, but have only numbed it.

We started down the road of repentance, but then we "hit the snooze button." By the time you read this, I wonder what else will have occurred.

Yes, my friend. There comes a time when we have to open our eyes. We have to let our Daddy take a look at our painful soar. We must stop clinching on to it and let our loving Father apply his healing salve to the wound.

As the result of one of the many times that the children of Israel sinned against G-d, fiery serpents of death came and bit them, killing many of them.

"Then they traveled from Mount Hor on the road toward the Sea of Suf in order to go around the land of Edom; but the people's tempers grew short because of the detour. The people spoke against G-d and against Moshe: 'Why did you bring us up out of Egypt? To die in the desert? There's no real food, there's no water, and we're sick of this miserable stuff we're eating!'

"In response, ADONAI sent poisonous snakes among the people; they bit the people, and many of Israel's people died. The people came to Moshe and said, 'We sinned by speaking against ADONAI and against you. Pray to ADONAI that he rid us of these snakes.' Moshe prayed for the people, and ADONAI answered Moshe: 'Make a poisonous snake and put it on a pole. When anyone who has been bitten sees it, he will live.'

"Moshe made a bronze snake and put it on the pole; if a snake had bitten someone, then, when he looked toward the bronze snake, he stayed alive." (B'midbar/Numbers 21:4-9)

Their sin had given the enemy the right to come in and kill them. (Holy Spirit give us the proper perspective on sin's empowerment of our enemy in our lives.)

G-d, our Abba Father, Daddy Father, didn't just sit on his throne and look down in disgust. He did not watch as a spectating Nero did when watching his Christian captives ripped to pieces by the lions.

"I take no pleasure in having the wicked person die, but in having the wicked person turn from his way and live. So repent! Turn from your evil ways!" (Yechezk'el/Ezekiel 33:11).

Therefore, G-d provided a way for Israel to escape this curse of death that came upon them. He had Moses make a brass serpent and put it on a pole. He then told everyone to look upon the "snake on a stick" so that they could be healed and live.

If they did not look at the "cure" which G-d had provided, then they would die from their wound.

If they would only look, believing that G-d would heal them as He said he would, they would be healed and live.

In like manner, Yeshua, our Saviour, became sin and was crucified on a tree.

"G-d made this sinless man be a sin offering on our behalf, so that in union with him we might fully share in G-d's righteousness." (2 Corinthians 5:21)

Yeshua is our "cure." He is the "snake on a stick" that provides the way for us to look and be healed.

"Just as Moshe lifted up the serpent in the desert, so must the Son of Man be lifted up; so that everyone who trusts in him may have eternal life." (Yochanan/John 3:14, 15).

Your Daddy in Heaven is reaching out to you in an effort to heal your wound. The wound, of course, being your sinful heart, which, if not tended to G-d's proper way, will die forever.

Have you called upon Yeshua to save you and heal you yet? Do so now! Do not hesitate. Tomorrow may never come. Those in the Twin Towers had no idea that 9/11 would be their last day.

"Therefore, as the Ruach Ha Kodesh says, Today if you hear G-d's voice, don't harden your hearts as you did in the Bitter Quarrel on that day in the Wilderness...Watch out, brothers, so that there will not be in any one of you an evil heart lacking trust, which could lead you to apostatize from the living G-d! Instead, keep exhorting each other every day, as long as it is called Today, so that none of you will become hardened by the deceit of sin." (Messianic Jews/Hebrews 3:7-13)

This brings us to another important point. Just as the unharmed hand rushes to the protection of the wounded hand, so do the other members of the body rush to the aid of the wounded member, or so they should. Right?

Yeshua tells us in the 25th chapter of Matthew that when he returns, he will set the sheep on his right and the goats on his left. Pay Attention! What do you think is going on in the world today?

"All the nations will be assembled before him, and he will separate people one from another as a shepherd separates sheep from goats. The 'sheep' he will place at his right hand and the 'goats' at his left.

"Then the King will say to those on his right, 'Come, you whom my Father has blessed, take your inheritance, the Kingdom prepared for you from the founding of the world: For I was hungry and you gave me food, I was thirsty, and you gave me something to drink, I was a stranger and you made me your

guest, I needed clothes and you provided them, I was sick and you took care of me, I was in prison and you visited me....Yes! I tell you that whenever you did these things for one of the least important of these brothers of mine, you did them for me!"

"Then he will also speak to those on his left, saying, 'Get away from me, you who are cursed! Go off into the fire prepared for the Adversary and his angels! For I was hungry and you gave me no food, thirsty and you gave me nothing to drink, a stranger and you did not welcome me, needing clothes and you did not give them to me, sick and in prison and you did not visit me...Yes! I tell you that whenever you refused to do it for the least important of these people, you refused to do it for me!"

"They will go off to eternal punishment, but those who have done what G-d wants will go to eternal life." (Mattityahu/Matthew 25:32-46)

Before you quote these verses to suggest that we need to feed the poor Muslims of the world whose rich leaders allow them to starve, let me enlighten you to the fact that it is G-d's people he is referring to. Yes, we are all called to be Good Samaritans to all people (search the New Covenant writings for that parable). But that also includes the historically hated Jewish people. What have you peoples of the world done with the Children of Promise? How have you treated Yeshua's brethren, the JEWS, in addition to the believers in Messiah?

Yes, it is good to help the poor Muslim Afghanis, but why aren't the oil rich "peaceful" nations of Islam doing this for their brothers? If they be so peaceful, why then aren't they leading the charge against terrorism? Because their hands are covered in blood and they desire the destruction of everyone who stands in the way of Allah, especially the Jews. Peace to those of you who bow to them, but death to those who dare stand in their way. "Death to Israel" is their cry!

YHVH PROMISED AVRAHAM, *"I will bless those who bless you, but I will curse anyone who curses you; and by you all the families of the earth will be blessed." (B'resheet/Genesis 12:3)*

When America turns against Israel, the G-d of Israel will turn against her. And that goes the same for any other nation that dares to come against G-d's anointed.

AND TO YITZ'CHAK (Isaac) YHVH PROMISED, *"Stay in this land, and I will be with you and bless you, because I will give all these lands to your descendants, and by your descendants all the nations of the earth will bless themselves. All this is because Avraham heeded what I said and did what I told him to do -- he followed my mitzvot, my regulations and my teachings." (B'resheet/Genesis 26:3-5)*

"...the land belongs to me -- you are only foreigners and temporary residents with me." (Vayikra/Leviticus 25:23)

THE LAND OF ISRAEL IS YHVH'S. IT IS NOT ISRAEL'S TO GIVE AWAY, NOR THE PALESTINIANS' TO TAKE AWAY. AND IT IS NOT FOR YOU NOR FOR THE U.N. TO DECIDE! IT IS YHVH'S AND HE WILL DECIDE! HE WILL NOT ALLOW IT TO BE TRADED FOR "PEACE."

"Here is what ADONAI says: 'If you can break my covenant with the day and my covenant with the night, so that daytime and nighttime no longer come when they are supposed to, then my covenant with my servant David also can be broken, so that he will not have a descendant to reign from his throne or L'vi'im who are cohanim to minister to me.

"To the degree that the armies of heaven are past counting and the sand by the sea past measuring, I will increase the descendants of my servant David and the L'vi'im ministering to me.'

"This word of ADONAI came to Yirmeyahu: 'Haven't you noticed that these people are saying, 'ADONAI has rejected the two families he chose'? Hence they despise my people and no longer look at them as a nation. Here is what ADONAI says:

"If I have not established my covenant with day and night and fixed the laws for sky and earth, then I will also reject the descendants of Ya'akov and of my servant David, not choosing from his descendants people to rule over the descendants of Avraham, Yis'chak and Ya'akov. For I will cause their captives to come back, and I will show them compassion." (Yirmeyahu/Jeremiah 33:20-26)

FLY BE FREE!

Did you ever see the Mork and Mindy show? The one with Robin Williams playing the alien who landed on earth in a space ship shaped like an egg? Did you see that one episode where he finds the carton of eggs and thinks they are his people in captivity? He picks one of the eggs up and then gently tosses it up saying, "Fly, be free!" as it drops into the sink with a splat.

What's that got to do with you and me? Nothing really. I just thought it was a humorous memory that might make Mork and Mindy fans smile. It also shows you my age and my childhood influences. Actually, the eggs have nothing to do with this chapter, but the "Fly, be free" part does.

We may not be eggs, but we are turkeys. Yes, we are all turkeys. G-d made us to be eagles, but we all fell into turkeyness and became turkeys.

I've heard various preachers use the turkey/eagle analogy and thought it would be a good one to build upon for this chapter. However, I'm going to take it from a different perspective.

There is a war being waged! A war between the Turkey world and the Eagle world. This world used to be pure Eagleness, but Turkeyness found its way into power through that Father of Turkeys, the Great Turkey, who now reigns over this once pure land.

We were all created to be Eagles. But Turkeyness mutated us into Turkeys. All are Turkeys now and unable to reach the land of Eagles. As much as we may try to convince ourselves that we are Eagles or try to act like Eagles we all fall short of the glory of Eagleland.

We can pluck our Turkey feathers and try to put Eagle feathers on, but we are still unable to reach Eagleland by our own efforts. Our "righteous" Eagle feathers will not raise us to the level of the Great Eagle.

Many try to act like an Eagle. We ask ourselves, "WWGED?" "What Would the Great Eagle Do?" But, this is not a valid question until we first meet the Great Eagle and are filled with the Great Eagle's Spirit.

Just as turkeys differ from eagles, likewise, so do the "unsaved" differ from the "saved" individuals who put their faith in the Messiah of mankind.

We must cease our efforts and admit that we are truly sinners filled with sinfulness that good works cannot hide. We must see that our need for salvation from sin can only come from another source other than ourselves. We must look for our redemption from the Son of Adam who lived without sin.

Thanks be to YHVH, our Father in Heaven. He has provided a way for us to be delivered from our sinfulness. Not only can he give us real "Eagle feathers," but He can make us into real "Eagles."

This was accomplished when the Father sent his Son, Yeshua (as his Hebrew mother called him), to earth as a human man. Yet, even though the Messiah was 100% man, and 100% G-d, he was a man without sin. He lived as a man, walked, ate, drank, slept, and suffered as a man, yet he did not give into sin as all other men have and as the evil one, Satan, desired.

The Devil, aka Lucifer, who is also the Father of Sinners, hates the Messiah with a passion. He did not like this intruder coming into his domain to bring aid to the sinners of sinful earth.

Remember, sinful earth used to be part of holy paradise. Mankind was not supposed to be in bondage to sin and the enemies of YHVH, but rather, pure and holy sons and daughters of the Living G-d, as he had originally designed. The Creator (not created) Messiah had come to earth as a human to lead mankind back into right standing with YHVH and into eternal life in heaven with him.

The Devil managed to blind the eyes of sinful man and stirred them against "this Turkey" who claimed to be the Messiah. The sinful ones, Jew AND Gentile, (who is without sin?), turned on the Messiah who came as a man and killed him. They had a party as they watched him "bake in the sun."

But death could not keep its grip upon this particular man. Although the Messiah had become a man, he did not allow sin to stain him.

As the Father in heaven had designed, the Messiah became not only a man, but he took upon the sinfulness of mankind upon the stake which the Father of Lies and his "children" had intended to "roast" our Salvation. (As mentioned before, Yeshua means salvation in Hebrew, thus the reason I choose to use his Hebrew name in this book as added emphasis to the very nature of his being, found in his Hebrew name.)

The aroma of the Messiah's sacrifice rose to the Father in heaven. Grief stricken as he was, the Father was greatly pleased in knowing that his son had now provided atonement for all sinful men. Now, all the sinners of sinful earth have a way to escape sin and the wages of sin, which is eternal death, but only if they put their trust in him.

"For what one earns from sin is death, but eternal life is what one receives as a free gift from G-d, in union with the Messiah Yeshua, our Lord." (Romans 6:23)

The Messiah had become a man and lived without sin, making him the ONLY one able to qualify as our atonement. He is our Pesach Lamb. Since he was executed for our sins, AND came back to life as the risen Messiah, we now have a way to reach heaven.

The Messiah now calls upon ALL mankind to look to him for redemption. Stop fluttering away with your efforts to reach heaven. The only way to The Father is through the Son.

"How?" you ask.

By faith! Faith in the Messiah! Call upon Him to deliver you from your sinfulness. He will then send his Spirit to you to make you into the holy disciple he calls you to be.

Pay attention!

The Spirit does not come to make us better sinners. He comes to make us into holy and pure believers. A believer is not a believer, unless the belief is lived out in the life of the believer. People today confuse intellectual acknowledgment with committed trust and obedience. To believe in the Messiah is to trust and obey him. Anything short is just empty lip-service.

We are 100% sinful and 0% holy before the Spirit of YHVH comes to us. There is not "an Eagle within us" waiting to be released. Sorry Oprah. But this just doesn't "fly" with G-d. (Pun intended.) There is nothing holy about us or within us. We are entirely sinful before being born again.

We cannot enter heaven with a stain of sinfulness upon us or within us. We must be changed 100% into saints before we will be allowed to enter YHVH's domain. And this is done without the Pope proclaiming it so. Our Father in Heaven is the one who gives sainthood, and it is given to ALL who call upon the Redeemer, Yeshua.

We must die to our sinfulness and be resurrected in holiness. THEN, we must reckon ourselves to be dead to sin and alive in righteousness, not by attitude, but by faith. We must be born again! When we call upon the Messiah to deliver us from our sin, He hears us and immediately sends his Spirit to make us into new creatures. He not only cleanses us, but he changes us totally.

The Messiah responds to our need, not our effort. He sees us as the Turkeys that we are and desires to make us the Eagles he meant for us to be. Our fluttering does not attract his attention. Our humbleness and contriteness is what gets his attention. So stop your fluttering and simply believe on him and call for his aid. He will not hesitate nor fail to find you.

His response to you is immediate! As soon as you call, his Spirit is there changing you into a holy priest citizen of heaven before you realize what has happened. Now comes the hard part. Learning to fly.

We have lived our entire lives as Turkeys in a sinful world. Now, after we have become a new creature, we find that the Turkeys around us are still Turkeys. And they don't like it now that we have become Eagles. Remember, the dark hates the light, no matter how nice you are to them. Uphold G-d's standard and you will be ridiculed, mocked, and even persecuted no matter how inoffensive you try to be.

A "funny" story - This one comes from a former associate Pastor of a wonderful church I attended in Lubbock, Texas. I'm not sure where he is now. Mel told us about a time shortly after his "transformation" into a new creature when he gave his life to

Yeshua. He was getting a ride from one of his old drug buddies. Mel was of the hippy generation. His friend was driving and toking on his joint. After taking a hit, he held it over to Mel and offered him a puff. Mel graciously declined with a thank you, and nothing more.

"Who the hell do you think you are preaching to me? You self-righteous @#%%@$%!"

It was something like that. All Mel said was "No, thanks." He didn't preach to his friend, but his friend new about Mel's transformation to life in Messiah. The darkness truly hates the light.

These unsaved sinners and their Father of sin realize that there is something different about us, but they insist that we are still sinners at heart and are destined to sinfulness until the day we die. They remind us constantly of our old sin ridden lives. Even though we know a change has occurred in ourselves, our minds still remember the old way of life.

The sad thing is that many of us believe the Father of Lies and the other sinners and we continue to act like sinners. Our minds have thought like sinners for so long and we still remember all our past experiences and we doubt... "Well...maybe they are right."

The reality is that once we have been "baked" with the Messiah, we no longer live, but He now lives in and through us. It's a mystery! Our beings have been changed. We are no longer sinners bound by sin. Now, we have become free by the power of the Holy Spirit, free from not only the wages of sin, but the power of sin itself.

The problem we now experience is within our minds. This is the battleground. The war is fought and won or lost within the minds of every person. It is lost when the sinner stays a sinner and won when the sinner becomes a believer, in thoughts AND deeds. Yet, the battle continues to wage even after we become followers of the Messiah.

Lucifer and his fallen cohorts hound us day and night. His army does not rest. They do not play fair nor care if we get hurt. As a matter of fact, they thirst for our blood even more when they see us hurt. Mercy is not in their vocabulary. They do not let up to allow us a breather. They are constantly on the attack because we become their enemy when we become committed to the Blessed Hope of Israel.

Notice, this is a spiritual war. I have not named any group of men or nation.

"Use all the armor and weaponry that G-d provides, so that you will be able to stand against the deceptive tactics of the Adversary. For we are not struggling against human beings, but against the rulers, authorities and cosmic powers governing this darkness, against the spiritual forces of evil in the heavenly realm. So take up every piece of war equipment G-d provides; so that when the evil day comes, you will be able to resist; and when the battle is won, you will still be standing." (Ephesians 6:11-13)

"For although we do live in the world, we do not wage war in a worldly way; because the weapons we use to wage war are not worldly. On the contrary, they have G-d's power for demolishing strongholds. We demolish arguments and every arrogance that raises itself up against the knowledge of G-d; we take every thought captive and make it obey the Messiah. And when you have become completely obedient, then we will be ready to punish every act of disobedience." (2 Corinthians 10:3-6)

The Father in Heaven did not call you to be a child of His so that you could immediately fly to Heaven and leave your fellow captives behind. He calls us to be his talmidim, disciples, and to turn to the sinners around us and help them to see what we have seen, to experience what we have experienced, to be free as we are now free.

The Messiah came to save all sinners, not just you and me. He wants to use us to get the message to the whole world. Remember, this is a war of the mind. Ideas rule the world. Belief systems are what make the world what it is. Does Bin Ladin and his Jihad not make my point even more clear here? How about the political correctness belief system that has recently swept the Western mind? What about the lie that all religions lead to G-d? The fact is that all religions outside of Yeshua's, lead AWAY from G-d. The reason they are so "similar" is because they come from the same source.

The Devil is this source of false religions. He is the Father of Lies. He fully understands this war of ideas and is a master at it. Hence, the title, Father of Lies. He knows he has lost the war. But, until the rest of the world realizes who the Victor is, he will not rest until every sinner dies a sinner after worshipping him all of their sinful lives.

That's why he tries to make us born again believers as useless as possible. He knows he has lost us to the Messiah when we call upon Yeshua to save us. The Messiah has rescued us from the Devil's nest. So, the Devil tries to keep us from helping other sinners to become committed followers of the Messiah.

Since he has lost the war over our beings, he tries to win the battle in our minds. He tries to keep us from soaring as Eagles. He wants us to walk like sinners and still think we are sinners until the Messiah comes to take us to our new home.

"Once a Turkey, always a Turkey!" he constantly reminds us.

"You can't fly. You're still a sinner deep down inside."

In the letter to the believers in Rome, Shaul (aka Paul) wrote, *"do not let yourselves be conformed to the standards of the 'olam hazeh, (world). Instead, keep letting yourselves be transformed by the renewing of your minds; so that you will know what G-d wants and will agree that what he wants is good, satisfying and able to succeed." (Romans 12:2)*

If any sinner is in the Messiah, he/she is no longer a sinner, but a holy citizen of Heaven. Our minds must stop thinking like sinners and start thinking like the free believers we now are.

Our ability to be the Eagles that we are can only come through our faith in the Messiah and the grace he gives us through his Holy Spirit.

In Titus, we are told, *"For G-d's grace, which brings deliverance, has appeared to all people. It teaches us to renounce godlessness and worldly pleasures, and to live self-controlled, upright and godly lives now, in this age; while continuing to expect the blessed fulfillment of our certain hope, which is the appearing of our Deliverer, Yeshua the Messiah. He gave himself up on our behalf in order to free us from all violation of Torah and purify for himself a people who would be his own, eager to do good." (Titus 2:11-14)*

If you are still a Turkey, or a sinner, and want to become an Eagle, or saved believer, then ask the Messiah, Yeshua, to save you from your sins and transform you into the new creature, he wants you to be. Ask him for forgiveness and receive it. Put the book down and ask him right now...

"Holy Yeshua, save me from my sins and the power of sin. Forgive me Father for my disobedience to your word. Make me a holy child of G-d, obedient to your word. Fill me with your Ruach Ha Kodesh, Holy Spirit, and give me understanding of these things. Teach me your ways so that I may teach others. In the name of Yeshua, Amen."

If you are a believer that is having trouble flying, ask G-d to forgive you for your unbelief and to help you believe. In Mark 9:24, YHVH heard the doubting father's prayer. He will hear yours with the same compassion. Put the book down now and ask him to forgive your unbelief and to teach you to fly...

Yesha'yahu/Isaiah 40:31 tells us, *"those who hope in ADONAI will renew their strength, they will soar aloft as with eagles' wings; when they are running they won't grow weary, when they are walking they won't get tired."*

TO SUFFER, OR NOT TO SUFFER?

So, before you meet the Messiah and put your faith and trust in him, are you a sinner under condemnation? Yes.

After you meet the Messiah and receive him, are you a sinner under condemnation? According to scripture, NO!

"Therefore, there is no longer any condemnation awaiting those who are in union with the Messiah Yeshua." (Romans 8:1)

Can a follower of Muhammad or any other religious leader claim such as we do in Messiah?

Then, why do we still condemn ourselves? Why do we walk in defeat? Why do we still consider ourselves cursed?

We live in a cursed world, but that does not mean we have to walk in condemnation! Through the Blood of Yeshua, we have the victory. Victory over what? Over eternal death! *"For what one earns from sin is death; but eternal life is what one receives as a free gift from G-d, in union with the Messiah Yeshua, our Lord." (Romans 6:23)*

Does this mean we won't die? No. Until the Messiah returns, we will all die the physical death and sleep with our ancestors until the resurrection. (1 Thessalonians 4:13-18)

Does this mean we won't get sick? No. Our physical bodies last only so many years. Sickness is a result of our body's immune system becoming too weak to fight off sickness. It is inevitable. Sickness and death are not necessarily a result of our personally displeasing G-d; it is a result of the fall of man. Do not confuse the two!

Don't misunderstand. When we sin, it does open us up to the enemy to bring sickness upon us. But don't equate ALL sickness and tragedy with your individual sins. Yet don't discount the possibilities. If you have done something wrong repent and confess it. Ya'akov, or James, tells us in chapter 5:13-16 to call the elders and pray for one another. In verse 15, he relates some sickness to sin, and repentance and prayer to healing.

There may be a connection and it should be investigated. But, do not automatically equate your relative's death from cancer to their lack of faith.

Unforgiveness and bitterness must also be taken into serious consideration. Often, this is the reason for "unexplained" suffering, especially when one appears to be "living right." You may not be "living in sin," but do you have "differences" with another person? Do not overlook this and do not ignore it. Unforgiveness is very destructive, sometimes more so than "sin" is. Not that it isn't a sin. It is a sin. But, like gossip, it is easily ignored. It is a leaven that destroys those who harbor it. Don't let your heart become a harbor for unforgiveness and bitterness.

Speaking of gossip. What a shame we Christians bring upon the name of Messiah. Why is it that those of us who "have Jesus in our hearts" are the first and worst when it comes to stabbing our neighbor in the back? For those of us who know it is wrong, why do we smile and laugh at the jokes and remarks that are unbefitting the presence of G-d? Does G-d not hear? Why is religion and G-d's praise unfit for the work place, while belittling and mockery are acceptable?

Many of you know what I am talking about. Why do we put up with it? I dare say it is because we fear man more than we fear G-d. I too am guilty of trying to be nice instead of saying enough is enough. Gone are the days of decency and innocence in our land. The norm is disrespect and mockery of our neighbor. There is little difference between the non-believer and the "professing believer" in the work place or the school ground.

What a shame and disgrace we, who "have Jesus in our heart," bring upon ourselves. Why is it a "crime" to stand for decency now a days? To refuse to participate in course jesting or other sins is "holier than thou" or "judgmental"? Why do you profess to be a Christian and then turn around and mock your brother or sister who is trying to obey G-d and live an upright life?

Gossip and disrespect are not the fruits of G-d-fearing people. We should not be ashamed to uphold G-d's standards in the public realm. However, my fear is that soon our freedom to do so will be stripped from us. We are to blame for this moral collapse in our society. We all have allowed the boundaries to be moved. Likewise, we will be held accountable if we do not attempt to restore them.

In addition, do not equate condoning sin with forgiveness. To uphold G-d's standards is not hateful and unforgiving. On the contrary, it is true love for G-d and Man when we obediently uphold G-d's instructions for living in both our deeds and our words. Our society and culture have forgotten this. If we do not raise the banner of righteousness, who will?

"Righteousness makes a nation great, but sin degrades any people." (Mishlei/Proverbs 14:34) (What WAS the secret to America's success? What IS the reason for her collapse?)

As I mentioned earlier, sin is the reason we have so much pain and suffering in this life. It rules over this world until the returning Messiah destroys it and this world with fire.

"Dear friends, I am writing you now this second letter; and in both letters I am trying to arouse you to wholesome thinking by means of reminders; So that you will keep in mind the predictions of the holy prophets and the command given by the Lord and Deliverer through your emissaries.

"First, understand this: during the Last Days, scoffers will come, following their own desires and asking, 'Where is this promised 'coming' of his? For our fathers have died, and everything goes on just as it has since the beginning of creation.'

"But wanting so much to be right about this, they overlook the fact that it was by G-d's Word that long ago there were heavens, and there was land which arose out of water and existed between the waters, and that by means of these things the world of that time was flooded with water and destroyed. It is by that same Word that the present heavens and earth, having been preserved, are being kept for fire until the Day of Judgment, when ungodly people will be destroyed. Moreover, dear friends, do not ignore this: with the Lord, one day is like a thousand years and a thousand years like one day. The Lord is not slow in keeping his promise, as some people think of slowness; on the contrary, he is patient with you; for it is not his purpose that anyone should be destroyed, but that everyone should turn from his sins. However, the Day of the Lord will come "like a thief."

On that Day the heavens will disappear with a roar, the elements will melt and disintegrate, and the earth and everything in it will be burned up." (2 Kefa/Peter 3:1-10)

There are those who teach that you do not have to get sick anymore. They say that G-d has "healed you by his stripes."

I may make some people mad here, but I must say that I don't know but of a few people mentioned in the Bible who did not see death. Sooner or later, our bodies will give up the breath of life and die. The vast majority will give it up via some kind of sickness or tragic accident.

If that teaching, of G-d wanting us to be free of sickness and tragedy is as some teach it, then something is terribly wrong in G-d's kingdom. Most of us probably aren't saved and we are fooling ourselves.

Again, don't misunderstand me. G-d hates sickness, pain, and suffering more than you and I do. But, until he destroys this world as mentioned above, sin and its destructive consequences will remain on this earth. This is a tricky subject that requires thorough study of G-d's word.

Suffice to say that "health and wealth" ARE associated with righteous living, and "sickness and poverty" ARE associated with sin. So, instead of passing laws "approving cloning and stem cell research," how about calling the nation back to righteousness, if you want to "heal our diseases," Mr. Congressman and Mr. President? It is a tragedy that righteousness is mockingly set aside as an "opinion" rather than upheld as a standard. Freedom is not what made us great. Righteousness as defined by YHVH is.

To the Law and the testimony...What does G-d say in his Word about death? Answer: *"From ADONAI'S point of view, the death of those faithful to him is costly." (Tehillim/Psalms 116:15)* And again, *"As I live, swears ADONAI Elohim, 'I take no pleasure in having the wicked person die, but in having the wicked person turn from his way and live." (Yechezk'el/Ezekiel 33:11)*

Also, we are told, *"The righteous person perishes, and nobody gives it a thought. Godly men are taken away, and no one understands that the righteous person is taken away from the evil yet to come." (Yesha'yahu/Isaiah 57:1)*

42

What does that tell you about G-d's heart towards death? We need to get our paradigm in line with G-d's. Before you look at the death and destruction that occurred on September 11, 2001 at the World Trade Center and the Pentagon, and events since then, consider those scriptures we just read. G-d alone knows our hearts, and G-d alone judges them to be righteous or wicked. When the wicked die, it is because they have spurned G-d too long and have used up their time. When the righteous die, it is for G-d's glory and his purposes. Those who die in Messiah look forward to that blessed hope of the resurrection at the last Shofar. Let us not lose sight of that in all the pain and suffering that we see in our world.

G-d's judgment is TRUE and JUST. Why do the preachers in our nation shrink back from this? G-d IS JUDGING AMERICA! HE IS JUDGING ALL NATIONS! Judgment is a blessing to the righteous, but a curse for the wicked. Read the story of Passover in the book of Sh'mot, or Exodus. G-d's judgment fell upon Egypt as he protected his people Israel. There was light in Goshen, while there was darkness in Egypt. The same Death Angel that took the firstborn of those without the covering of the lamb's blood "passed over" those with the LAMB's blood covering.

The bottom line is this. If you or someone you love is sick, dies in an accident, or just has "bad luck" in life, that does not mean that you are hated by G-d and that G-d is punishing you or them. Sin is punishing this world. G-d seeks to redeem us and to save us from the ultimate punishment = the second death. (Revelation 20:4-14)

There are two deaths and two resurrections. Except for those alive at the Messiah's return, all experience the first death which is physical death. The second death, which is spiritual death, is for those who reject Yeshua (Salvation).

The first resurrection is the one at Messiah's return when the "eagles" are raised and reign with Christ for 1000 years. The second resurrection is the one where the wicked dead are raised, only to find judgment awaiting them and then they receive the second death as their sentence.

If you truly believe that G-d considers us to be sinning or without faith because we are poor or suffer in this world, then I challenge you to prove it with your own life. Go to Central and South America, Africa, Russia, and China and preach this doctrine. Better yet, go outside and across town to the "poor" side. Drive down to the section where we don't want to go at night.

Remember Yeshua's warning to the Messianic community in Laodicea. (Revelation 3:14-22) Prosperity does not necessarily equate to G-d's blessings. The drug cartels are filthy rich, but that's why they are called "filthy." They got rich through murder, greed, and all manners of filthy sin.

Go up in the backwoods of America and see if this "prosperity" doctrine works. I call it false doctrine! It is more damaging to G-d's people than sin itself. Because, other than encouraging "lust of the eyes, lust of the flesh, and the boastful pride of life," it disillusions G-d's people and causes many to fail at that which G-d has called them to do with their lives. Little setbacks become walls unable to climb. The lie becomes truth. That which is not becomes so. That which they can becomes that which they can't. "G-d can use me" becomes, "G-d can't use me." "G-d wants to use me" becomes, "G-d won't use me."

Why? "Because I'm not perfect and I'm suffering. If I'm suffering, I must be displeasing to G-d. If I'm displeasing to G-d, then I must be sinning against G-d. If I'm sinning against G-d, I cannot be used and blessed by G-d." Yeshua learned obedience through suffering. Let us be careful about our words and definitions.

Now, don't take me wrong. Miracles can and do happen. But, miracles aren't the norm, (yet). I don't understand why G-d performs miracles when he does, or doesn't perform them when he doesn't. G-d is G-d. How can we understand His ways? Back to the Bible. "To the Law and the Testimony."

YHVH sees what we don't see. He has his reasons. Who are we that we have to know all and see all? Does G-d need our permission to act? Does he even need our request?

I have a friend who is a missionary in Guatemala. In 1998, I was over in South Korea teaching conversational English. We were sharing our experiences via email. What an amazing accomplishment for mankind... Email!

Contrary to what you might think of South Korea, it is very much like America in its technology and standard of living. In Seoul, McDonald's, Burger King, KFC, Pizza Hut, Baskin Robbins are everywhere. And when you ride the train around town at night, you see neon crosses all over the city. The country is about half Christian. They have more churches on more street corners than I've seen in American cities in the "Bible-belt."

Anyway, I was asking my friend if he had experienced any miracles down there in Guatemala. I hadn't seen any activity in Seoul. I heard about Shamans in the villages, but no miracles to mention in the churches. Not that they didn't occur, I just hadn't come across any.

He's a very modest and meek individual. He didn't sensationalize anything. He hinted to some things happening, but only shared one story after I kept bugging him to share one with me.

Finally, he told me about this young four year old boy. My friend was helping in a medical outreach in an Indian village. While there, this little boy was carried in by his grandmother. He had never walked. He was in a semi-unconscious state most of the time and had to be spoon fed. My friend saw the doctor bend the boy's legs like garden hoses because of the lack of muscle and bone development. The doctor said there was nothing they could do but pray for the child.

Pray? The group with my friend did just that. After about 15 minutes of prayer, the child's eyes rolled down and he began looking around the room. Fifteen minutes later, the child sat up. After another 30 minutes, the child actually stood up for the first time in his life and was moving around.

"There was great rejoicing and several people put their faith in the Messiah at that time," said my friend.

This is why I believe miracles happen. Just as in the time he was on the earth, Yeshua performed miracles not only to glorify the Father in Heaven, but to meet the real needs of the people. Yeshua touches peoples' lives. He meets their needs. He doesn't just show off his power, he answers their prayers. And he will answer yours if you humble yourself and call upon his name.

During his time on earth, he healed the lame, sick, blind, and demon possessed. The woman with the blood disease was healed. The blind man was given his sight. The hungry were fed with real food.

As Yesha'yahu proclaimed of the Messiah, *"Then the eyes of the blind will be opened, and the ears of the deaf will be unstopped; then the lame man will leap like a deer, and the mute person's tongue will sing....Those ransomed by ADONAI will return and come with singing to Tziyon, on their heads will be everlasting joy. They will acquire gladness and joy, while sorrow and sighing will flee." (Yesha'yahu/Isaiah 35:5, 6, 10)*

Yeshua the Messiah did not make a statue of a cow to drink milk to show off his power. He gave the people food to fill their need and show his power. Miracles of G-d meet the need of the people in a tangible way. Compare the miracles of Yeshua in the Bible to the "miracles" of today that some proclaim to be of G-d. Are people being healed or awed? Are people receiving G-d's power or promises of G-d's power in the form of trinkets in exchange for "seed money" or penance?

Signs and wonders are truly wondrous. But, let me warn you my friends to be careful of seeking signs or accepting "miracles" in the name of G-d. Yes, Yeshua, through the Holy Spirit, still performs miracles, but beware of the enemy's power to perform signs and wonders.

I, for one, believe in miracles. I've not experienced any first hand, yet. I know people like my friend who have.

Without getting side tracked and off course, let me just warn you of the devil's deception. Remember, Satan is an angel of light. He loves to imitate G-d and take the glory. That was his original sin. He wanted G-d's place. He still wants G-d's place. He loves to get the glory and give G-d the blame. He doesn't want to do away with religion or even Christianity. He wants to take it away and rule over it as the "Messiah" of the world. BEWARE!!!

Are people getting saved? Praise G-d! But, salvation of souls does not mean the miraculous activities are of G-d. Another friend of mine told me once of a "healer" that came into town. He knew for a fact that this "healer" preacher was a fake, but miracles did take place in peoples' lives and souls were saved. My friend made a very good point. "It wasn't the preacher that performed the miracles; it was the faith of those praying people that G-d responded to." Even Paul made mention of those who preach out of greedy intentions, yet, none the less, he rejoiced in the Gospel being preached.

So, be careful, my friends. They say souls are being saved. Good. But, are they being grounded in the word of G-d? Is the doctrine sound? The Devil loves to put on a show. He loves to perform wonders in the name of G-d. He especially loves to lead people astray with the poison that comes along with it. He wants to be the world's "Messiah." He doesn't want to do away with the Messiah; he just wants to replace him.

I'm not pointing fingers at any ministry or minister. I'm just raising a voice of concern to the Body of Messiah. Be careful who you listen to, especially as the day of His return approaches.

"Everything I am commanding you, you are to take care to do. Do not add to it or subtract from it. If a prophet or someone who gets messages while dreaming arises among you and he gives you a sign or wonder, and the sign or wonder comes about as he predicted when he said, 'Let's follow other gods, which you have not known; and let us serve them,' you are not to listen to what that prophet or dreamer says. For ADONAI your G-d is testing you, in order to find out whether you really do love ADONAI your G-d with all your heart and being. You are to follow ADONAI your G-d, fear him, obey his mitzvot, listen to what he says, serve him and cling to him;" (D'varim/Deuteronomy 12:32-13:5)

Just because "G-d is given glory and praise," does not necessarily mean that G-d is behind the miracles. In Revelation 13, we are warned about the second beast that performs "signs and wonders."

"It performs great miracles, even causing fire to come down from heaven onto the earth as people watch. It deceives the people living on the earth by the miracles it is allowed to perform in the presence of the beast, and it tells them to make an image

honoring the beast that was struck by the sword but came alive again. It was allowed to put breath into the image of the beast, so that the image of the beast could even speak; and it was allowed to cause anyone who would not worship the image of the beast to be put to death." (Rev 13:13-15)

At the risk of offending my fellow Americans, look at the approval rating President George W. Bush had after the Terrorist attack on the World Trade Center. He had an 80+% approval rating while preaching about the greatness of Islam and Allah. Those who spoke against this acceptance of Allah as equal to the G-d of Abraham, Isaac, and Israel were ridiculed by the press and even rebuked by the President himself. Even the son of Billy Graham, Franklin Graham, was rebuked for speaking the truth.

If the nations can be so supportive of such a man, who claims to be a Christian, while preaching the words of Islam, how much more so will the "beast" be honored and adored for his great words and deeds that will bring "peace, signs and wonders" to the world? If President George W. Bush can mislead so many, how much easier will it be for the one inspired by the Angel of Light to deceive the world?

By the way, I voted for George W. Bush four times, twice as my Governor when I resided in Texas, and twice to be my President. I respect the man greatly, but he is not Yeshua! Nor is he less prone to deception than you or I. President Barack Obama is no greater a man than any other President before him and no less prone to deception than them either. G-d warned us that the vast majority of the world will be deceived and the great apostasy would occur. Why then is this so hard to acknowledge?

Sorry if this offends you, but if G-d didn't want us to be aware of this, he wouldn't have made it such a big deal by having John write it to us in the last book of the Bible with blessings for those who read it and curses for those who mess with it. (Rev 22:6-19)

"Pay attention! I am sending you out like sheep among wolves, so be as prudent as snakes and as harmless as doves. Be on guard...." (Mattityahu/Matthew 10:16)

"Do all you can to present yourself to G-d as someone worthy of his approval, as a worker with no need to be ashamed,

because he deals straightforwardly with the Word of the Truth....The Lord knows his own, and, let everyone who claims he belongs to the Lord stand apart from wrongdoing." (2 Tim 2:15-19)

Standing apart from wrongdoing includes refusing to proclaim falsehood for the sake of national or international unity.

Does former President Bush or President Obama, or any other, profess faith in Yeshua? Good. Does he proclaim Allah and Islam as good? Then he deceives those who listen to him. Follow him as he follows Messiah, and no further!

Listen to me Body of Messiah. You must awaken if you haven't yet. DO NOT BE DECEIVED!

"Don't let anyone deceive you in any way. For the Day will not come until AFTER THE APOSTASY has come AND the man who separates himself from Torah has been revealed, the one destined for doom.....When this man who avoids Torah comes, the Adversary will give him the power to work all kinds of false miracles, signs and wonders. He will enable him to deceive, in all kinds of wicked ways, those who are headed for destruction because they would not receive the love of the truth that could have saved them. This is why G-d is causing them to go astray, so that they will believe the Lie. The result will be that all who have not believed the truth, but have taken their pleasure in wickedness, will be condemned." (2 Thessalonians 2:3-12)

IS IT WORTH IT?

Is it worth it? "Is it worth what?" you ask.

Is it worth the effort? Is it worth the pain? They say, "No Pain, No Gain."

But is the pain worth it?

"I'm cursed! You're cursed! We're all cursed!"

"Actually, I think I'm the only one that is cursed. Every time I try, something goes wrong. I can't do anything right."

"When things start to look like they are getting better, G-d throws a stick in my wheel."

"G-d is punishing me."

Ever felt this way? Know anyone who does?

I've felt this way many times. I know many others that do too. I want you to know that you're not alone. Maybe you are one of those who have it made. It's just hunky dory with you. You don't know what "their" problem is. "Just get over it," you say.

Easier said than done.

In the midst of my words of warning and call to repentance, I hope I can encourage someone today. That's why I'm writing in such an informal way. Maybe I am sharing too much and making some of you uncomfortable.

I hope I am. I want you to "get over it." But, we can only get over it when we face it and deal with it.

G-d is not out to destroy you or make you suffer. Suffering is a part of this life, but G-d is not the source.

Allow me to share some of my deepest scars. This is where your "friendship" with me comes to bear. I hope you will not be offended by my honesty and candor.

I'm sure you have had different experiences than I have. But, I hope you will find something you can relate to in my words.

Some years ago at Christmas time, shortly after my divorce, I sat down with my kids and had a chat. This is when I learned about their mother telling them we "had" to split up. My son and daughter thought that I had to leave. Their mother had told them that we couldn't live together anymore and that is why I had to leave.

I'm sure they're mad at me for leaving since I left. That's ok. I don't blame them. At their age, what are they to think and feel?

I informed them that we did not "have" to split up. "I never wanted to leave you guys or your mother," I told them. "Your mother 'wanted' to split up, not me."

I was willing to work things out, but their mother, who was still "in the closet" at the time, was not. A year later I found out why.

My ex-wife believes that "G-d made her gay" and that she "couldn't live a lie anymore." No. It hasn't been easy. How do you deal with it? I have learned...one day at a time, and only with G-d's help.

My son, tried to hide his face. He didn't want me to see the tears that were welling up in his eyes. My daughter was almost 7 back then. Yet, she was so mature for her age and able to express herself. She amazes me still. She described the feeling she was having at that time as "a lump in her throat."

"Do you ever feel that way, Daddy?" she asked.

"Yes, I do right now sweetie," I responded.

My children were confused. They hurt, but didn't know how to express themselves. Like my daughter said, she wants her mommy and daddy. Yet, she knew she couldn't have both. Kids are very smart. But, they, like us adults, don't know how to deal with such conflicting emotions.

I asked my son why his eyes were tearing up. He said, because he doesn't like his mother for making me leave.

Understandable! Don't you think?

Not just the feelings towards his mother, but also towards me for leaving. They never understood why I "left." They are just now starting to grow in their understanding of many things. Eventually, they will decide which path they will take in life. They love their parents. It's not easy choosing one over the other.

Many of us don't realize the reality of the consequences of our decisions. Not just the hurt of the divorced parents, but especially of the children caught in the middle.

Can you see why G-d HATES divorce? G-d hates for his people to hurt and suffer!

Yeshua learned obedience through suffering. Not from his sin, but the sin of others. Unlike you and me, he suffered for the sins of others.

"Even though he was the Son, he learned obedience through his sufferings. And after he had been brought to the goal, he became the source of eternal deliverance to all who obey him, since he had been proclaimed by G-d as a cohen gadol to be compared with Malki-Tzedek." (Messianic Jews/Hebrews 5:8-10)

G-d's people have suffered throughout history. Suffering is part of life in this sinful world. Is suffering G-d's will for anyone? No! Suffering of any kind is not G-d's design.

Suffering is the result of mankind's sin and rebellion against G-d's perfect will. Earthquakes, tornadoes, hurricanes, droughts, floods, disease, all kinds of tragedies; these have been called "acts of G-d," or more recently, "results of global warming."

They are not results of global warming and they are not acts of G-d! These are results of sin....Mankind's sin! Yours and mine! We bring these things upon our heads.

Our sin empowers the enemy, Lucifer, aka Satan, and his comrades, to bring death, destruction, and suffering into our lives. Lucifer then turns and blames G-d for these tragedies. He tries to turn our confidence in our Messiah into doubt. Don't fall for this trick! Until the Messiah returns, suffering will continue. Contrary to the "prosperity" teachings in some of today's churches, suffering will be a part of every person's life. Death will meet all except for those alive at the Messiah's return. To understand the powerful destruction of sin, read Jeremiah.

As I stated before, the topic of sin and suffering is a tricky one. You must ground yourself in Torah, G-d's instructions, to understand G-d's heart about the matter. And even when you can't make sense of it, you are to trust YHVH, for that is the very definition of faith.

During the U.S. bombing in Afghanistan shortly after 9-11-2001, I saw news footage of young children being dug out of the rubble, covered with dirt, their precious lives taken away by stray bombs. With the love for my own children, I can only imagine the pain those parents must've felt. We never saw the news channels show the bodies, or pieces of bodies, from the World Trade Center. From the sound of the critics, maybe those who sympathize with the terrorists should've seen the bodies and blood that our NYC rescue and recovery workers saw.

Anyway, the death and destruction is hard to deal with, especially when innocent "bystanders" are killed in war. What despair to see your loved ones taken in such ways, no matter which side you are on.

Pain of the heart is painful, no matter what the cause or the place.

Regarding divorce, G-d hates to see two people tear apart what G-d has brought together. G-d hates to see the tears of the children who are torn between the two people they love most in life. It's not fair!

One day, as I was grieving in my heart over the agony of my own painful situation, I was crying to G-d asking if he even had ears or eyes. Why couldn't he see or hear my cries of pain?

His response was unexpected...no matter what your pain is inside your aching heart, to you and me, the Father says,

"My tears are more than yours. My cry is louder than yours. My pain is greater than yours. You do not see ALL that I see. My heart aches with you my child. I see what you see. I hear what you hear. Your pain is my pain. I told you I would always be with you and I am. I am right there by your side every moment. I weep with you. My angels are there to comfort you. Trust in me. I will make a new heaven and earth without tear or pain. I will wipe away the tears and restore the broken hearted. Trust in me. I will not forsake you."

To the children out there, whatever your age is now, in your teens or in your prime. It's not your fault! And it is ok to be angry with both of your parents! We must forgive, but we must first admit the pain. It is also ok to love both of your parents!

It is ok to feel more than one emotion at a time. You can feel all the emotions you are feeling. It is ok to get a "lump" in your throat, because you don't know which way to feel. Let yourself feel sad, happy, angry, excited, and whatever else you may be feeling or have felt in the past. What you feel is not evil or wrong! How you are "supposed" to feel is exactly how you feel right now. Let yourself feel what you feel. (Rage is not a feeling. Rage is a reaction. To feel pain is different than attempting to deal with that pain through acts of sinful anger.)

Kids never, NEVER want their parents to split up. As bad as things can get, they love their parents.

Are only adults allowed to feel hurt and rejected?

Feelings and perceptions are important. Your feelings. My feelings. Her feelings. His feelings. Perceptions influence our feelings.

Did you hear about the man on the subway with his children? He was just sitting there, staring away as if he were alone. His kids were getting rowdy and disturbing the others around them.

People were getting irritated and wondering where he learned his parenting skills. A couple folks were so irritated that they got up and went to the next car.

Finally, someone asked if something was wrong.

The man came to his senses and noticed what was going on. He was so apologetic. He explained to the person who inquired that his wife had just passed away. The children were too young to understand. But he was having a hard time with it.

Those around felt their hearts drop. Their perception of the man was far from accurate. They now had a new perspective of the man.

Don't we do that often? We perceive things one way although they may not be so.

Are you ready for this one?

King Saul of Israel had a very bad perception problem. His was one of severe proportions. If you've read his story, I'm sure you will understand where I'm coming from.

He felt depressed and paranoid. But it wasn't always the case. His problems began when he wavered in his faith and became more interested in what others thought. The interests of his nation became more important than the interests of his G-d. (Sound familiar?) He was ordered by Samuel to wait for him. But, Saul became impatient and went on with the sacrifices without Samuel. (I Samuel 13).

Because of his disobedience to G-d, Saul had the kingdom taken away from him. Not right away, but later, someone else would replace him.

Saul knew he'd done wrong.

Have you been disobedient to G-d? Do you feel like G-d is against you? Sure, you are probably feeling the consequences of your actions. But, does this mean G-d is against you?

Saul let jealousy consume him. David had come into the picture and was eventually chosen to replace him. This infuriated Saul.

Murder entered his mind. He tried more than once to kill David and did kill others he felt threatened him.

"Conspiracy!" Saul had certain priests that he thought were conspiring against him slaughtered.

What's Saul got to do with us today?

Well, let me bring it closer to home.

Have you heard the term, "going postal?"

Yes, I'm talking about the violence that seems to be erupting more often in our headlines.

I don't know everyone's situation. But, I believe that desperation to the point of killing others in our society is an intense cry for help, albeit, a wrong way to cry for help. Those who commit such acts aren't the only ones crying for help. For each one of those who take their "cry" to this end, there are countless others who are on their way to a miserable end.

By no means do I agree with or justify the violent attacks people have made on others, especially in the name of G-d.

But what drives people to this point of no return?

"No one being tempted should say, 'I am being tempted by G-d.' For G-d cannot be tempted by evil, and G-d himself tempts no one. Rather, each person is being tempted whenever he is being dragged off and enticed by the bait of his own desire. Then, having conceived, the desire gives birth to sin; and when sin is fully grown, it gives birth to death.

"Don't delude yourselves, my dear brothers -- every good act of giving and every perfect gift is from above, coming down from the Father who made the heavenly lights; with him there is neither variation nor darkness caused by turning. Having made

his decision, he gave birth to us through a Word that can be relied upon, in order that we should be a kind of firstfruits of all that he created.

"Therefore, my dear brothers, let every person be quick to listen but slow to speak, slow to get angry; for a man's anger does not accomplish G-d's righteousness!" (Ya'akov/James 1:13-20)

Your pain is real. My pain is real. Their pain is real. But, how we deal with our pain is up to us.

Many want to put the blame on others. "I was abused." "My father was an alcoholic." "They foreclosed on me unfairly." "I shouldn't have been fired." "They didn't give me a chance." "My father and mother didn't love me." "I was discriminated against." "The devil made me do it." "Society drove me to it." "My medication wasn't right."

And the list goes on. Maybe you've heard many more. Maybe you use a different one. Let's be honest with ourselves. Haven't we all tried to excuse away our shortcomings at times, whether they be big or small?

We must take responsibility for our actions. As intense as our pain may be, there is a Doctor who can help. The Great Physician is ready and willing, but he will not force you to seek his aid. You must come to him on your own free will. When you do, he will heal you as only he can.

Divorce. Maybe you haven't experienced this. I hope you haven't. Although you may not have, I hope you will read this and try to gain an understanding about those of us who have.

As I just mentioned, G-d hates divorce!!! Divorce is evil. Yet, it is on the rise in our society and even in our churches. Our nation is in a sad state when it comes to marriage and divorce. I heard recently that divorce in the church has surpassed that outside the church. What a sad witness! Is there no more shame?

Yes, I am divorced. And I still think it is evil. (As if what I think matters. G-d says he hates it!) For some, it is worse than the death of loved ones. I was on the rejected end of the divorce, which is why I can sympathize with those who describe it as worse than death. I can't relate to the one who does the rejecting, so I hope I can handle this with delicacy.

I mean no disrespect to you who recently lost a loved one, but I've lost people close to me too. As I mentioned earlier, my own father passed away recently. This statement does not lessen your pain. It only reveals the measure of pain felt by others. So please understand what I am saying about the pain felt inside that comes from divorce.

I considered myself to be a devout Christian. I thought my ex-wife was too. She claimed to be.

It was just before Easter. We were having trouble for some time. She used our financial situation as the smoke screen and justification for her desire to separate. "Irreconcilable differences." Is that really an excuse for Christians? Or just an attempt to rationalize selfishness and other sin?

Finally, she told me she didn't love me and wanted a divorce.

Heartbroken, I spent that Easter, (before discovering the richness of the Feast of Pesach, Passover), with my kids visiting one of my older brothers and his in-laws for the weekend. My boy was 5 and my girl was 3 at the time. What do you tell children?

I was broke and without a "real" job. None of my business ideas were working out. I was substitute teaching and searching for "real" work, but that "wasn't good enough," so I was told. So, I went to live with my mother. (Understand my appreciation for her?)

What started out to be only a couple months turned into a couple years. "Luckily," I found a Divorce Care group that helped enormously. If you are divorced, find a Divorce Care group, even if you have to drive a ways to it.

It is hard to put into words all that I would like to say, but I will trust the Lord to help me say what is needed for this time.

My "ex-to-be" was not totally open with me. I discovered in time that she had been struggling with the deception of homosexuality. I had my suspicions the year prior to our divorce. But it wasn't until "Ellen" came out on television, months after our divorce, that she did too. "G-d wanted her to be gay and divorce me...She could not continue living a lie."

Funny, I thought G-d said that no one should tear apart a marriage that he brought together.

During that first summer away from my "ex-to-be" wife and kids, I must have cried a tub of tears. I prayed and prayed, "believing" that G-d would work it out in my favor. After all, I was the "straight" Christian.

I tried to talk my "ex-to-be" into working things out, but she had made up her mind. Although I knew she was hiding the truth, I tried to reconcile. Her lies made it even harder to handle. Having to try and explain to two young children that which I did not understand was even harder.

I remember waking in the middle of the night often that summer. One night I had a terrible dream. It was still dark outside, before 5:00 a.m. I could sleep no more. I could stay in bed no more. I got up and went jogging. I was so angry, I ran a good distance and still did not feel any better afterwards.

After conversations with my ex-to-be. After her attacks and guilt trips she would impose upon me for leaving town and going back to my mother's, I would be so upset that I had to leave the house. My faith in G-d was put to the test and I admit I was near casting it aside, more than once.

My mother let me cry on her shoulder more than once. She herself had experienced rejection. My dad left only a few years prior, for different reasons. He was obsessed with money, which he didn't have much of, and alcohol, which he had too much of.

The reasons may be different, but the pain is the same.

I'm sure she had a hard time with me there, but isn't that what family is all about. How about the family of G-d?

At first, I was confident that G-d would stand by me and allow me to have my kids. But, time passed by. Things didn't go as I had prayed for them to. G-d didn't like my way. Maybe, G-d didn't like me.

I remember walking across the street to my old elementary school. I would walk to the middle of the big school yard and proceed to silently scream at G-d. Sometimes I wasn't so silent.

"What do you want from me?"

"Why are you doing this?"

"Why won't you speak to me? You sorry @#%*."

Yes, I cursed G-d more than once. I do not excuse it nor encourage it. I only admit it to show you my own sinful humanity. I urge you not to curse G-d as I did. Do not sin as I did and raise your fist against G-d in Heaven. DO CRY to G-d and raise your hands to him with prayers and petitions! But do not gnash your teeth with angry words and raised fists against the Holy and Just Creator G-d.

"I must be cursed. G-d is punishing me. What have I done to deserve this?"

One night, I was in the school yard with my fist in the air challenging G-d to kill me. "Smush me like a bug. What are you waiting for? Come on! Get it over with! Kill me! What is the sense in continuing like this?!"

A still small voice responded. Not audible, just that little voice in your head that you know is not you.

"I'm not a man that I can be provoked," He said.

Silence.

....

What do you think? How would you feel at that moment?

Shock was my first response. He actually responded.

Fear was my second. I must have struck a chord.

Relief was my third. I'm glad G-d is not a man that is so ruled by emotion and easily stirred to irrational behavior. The words of Hosea come to mind, *"I will not give vent to the fierceness of my rage...for I am G-d, not a human being"* (Hoshea/Hosea 11:9)

What next?

I stood there, eyes fixed to the stars above. Wondering what G-d's perspective is on things. No great secret was revealed to me. My circumstances had not changed one bit. But, a strange peace that passes understanding came over me. Isn't there a scripture that mentions peace that is beyond comprehension?

Another night of agony occurred sometime later. Again, I was angry and walked over to the school yard.

I proceeded to gnash my teeth and raise my fist to G-d again.

This time I heard another voice. It was another non-audible "thought" voice. Same accent as the one before. Sounded like my own thoughts. Makes you wonder, doesn't it? Are all our thoughts really our thoughts?

This one was not of G-d. How do I know? The "angel of light" had come to me this time offering to "help" me if I would only ask.

Anger filled me. "Get behind me Satan," I said. "I will not bow my knee to you. I may not understand G-d right now and hate what I see, but I will not submit to you! G-d, help me!"

Gone....

Like the temptation of Yeshua in the wilderness. Gone. Satan, or one of his subordinates more likely, came to tempt me into giving them a chance. Remember, they live for these moments and try to trick us into blaming G-d for our problems and turning against Him.

I know enough to understand that Satan is no friend to man. Contrary to the teachings of some, Satan is not your friend!

He is Lucifer, the angel that once stood in the presence of G-d. He was created perfect and good, as all G-d's creation was.

He and all the angels were given free will like you and I. Yet, he allowed pride to come in and sinned against G-d. He wanted, and still wants to be in G-d's place. He wants to be in your and my heart as well as in heaven. He can't be in more than one place, for he is not like G-d. But he still wants ownership of our hearts, our loyalty and our submission.

The real enemy is not in the abortion clinics. Nor in the government.

The enemy is all around us and the battlefield is the mind. Our mind is where we wage war. The hearts and minds of all are the battlegrounds for the souls of mankind.

Conspiracy? Many laugh at the idea. The media has done a fine job of making conspiracy theories a joke.

But, they are no joke! They are everywhere. You don't think there is a conspiracy in the world? They are everywhere on every level. Who's laughing at whom? You jest at the "Great Conspiracy?" You are clueless and a fool if you do.

People conspire how to steal the test answers for the upcoming final. Some conspire how they can steal their competitor's information or take them over. Some conspire how to commit a petty crime. Some conspire how to steal another country's secrets. Conspiracies go on every day, since the beginning of time.

The Conspiracy of all conspiracies that few are willing to discuss, or even acknowledge its existence, is that of Satan's design. Will Chris Matthews ever take this on Hardball (show on MSNBC)? Will Bill O'Reilly take it seriously (show on FoxNews)? Don't count on it. They might touch it for a few minutes, but in their arrogance and ignorance, they will claim to know more than G-d and mislead their viewers into discounting it as they usually do on religious topics.

Do you think that the Illuminati, as real as they were and may be, are Lucifer's equal? They like all other powerful organizations in the world are just pawns in Lucifer's plan. Do you really think Bin Laden is/was the top of the chain? Do you think he is the only one or last one to be used? Do you think he even realizes how small a pawn he is/was in the great scheme of things?

The human powers that be, at whatever level, high or low, do not know what or who they are dealing with. Many think they are doing "good" for the world. Their leader, Lucifer, has even convinced them that he is their friend and will reward them for their loyalty. "Paradise for martyrdom," is one example.

Look at the EU and the UN, for example, in addition to all the "kingdoms" of this world. See how they flex their muscle now. Are they really in charge? You haven't seen anything yet. They are mere pawns in the Conspiracy of conspiracies.

G-d says the wages of sin is death.

Lucifer, also known as Satan, will give them their paycheck. He will fulfill his promise of rewarding them with their severance pay when he is done using them for his purposes. Even when they think they are on top, when Lucifer is through with them, he discards them like any tyrant who has no more need for their services.

See now how the militant Muslims are being "dealt with." After they are "neutralized," who will be next? Dare I say, "America?" Who else stands in the way of the New World Order? Who's neutralizing who? The America we all love and cherish has come to her end. If she will not bow the knee to the Prince of this New World Order, she will be forced. Want proof? Read the following:

"We will have a world government whether you like it or not. The only question is whether that government will be achieved by conquest or consent." – James Paul Warburg, in 1950 before the U.S. Senate Committee on Foreign Relations

"We are likely to do better by building our house of World Order from the bottom up rather than the top down. An end-run around national sovereignty, eroding it piece by piece, is likely to get us to World Order faster than the old fashioned frontal assault." – Richard Gardner, former U.S. Deputy Assistant Secretary of State, in Foreign Affairs magazine, April 1974

"We are moving toward a New World Order, the world of Communism. We shall never turn off that road." – Mikhail Gorbachev in 1987

"We have before us the opportunity to forge for ourselves and future generations, a New World Order, a world where the rule of law, not the law of the jungle, governs the conduct of nations. When we are successful, and we will be, we have a real chance at this New World Order, an order in which a credible United Nations can use its peacekeeping role to fulfill the promise and vision of the U.N.'s founders" – President George Bush Sr., January 16, 1991 speech to the nation.

"In the 21st Century, national sovereignty will cease to exist and we will all answer to a single global authority." – Strobe Talbott, former U.S. Deputy Secretary of State under President Clinton, now President of the Brookings Institute, stated in July 1992 in Time Magazine. (By the way, Susan Rice, at time of this writing, serves as the U.S. Ambassador to the U.N. for President Obama. She worked under Strobe Talbott when she was at the Brookings Institute.)

"We are on the verge of a global transformation. All we need is the right major crisis and the nations will accept the new world order." – David Rockefeller, before the U.N. Business Council in 1994.

In December of 2000, shortly after the election of George W. Bush, Mikhail Gorbachev wrote an open letter, addressed to the new President, but obviously written to the American Public. I originally found this letter posted in the archives of the Dallas Morning News, but I believe it first posted on the Washington Post. I'm sure you can do a web search to find the whole article. It is worth looking up and reading in its entirety.

The article is titled, *"U.S. can't continue to act as a war victor."* In this article, I find one particular portion to be of great importance to highlight for you here.

"Globalization is a given - but "American globalization" would be a mistake. In fact, it would be something devoid of meaning and even dangerous. I would go even further and say it is time for America's electorate to be told the blunt truth: that the present situation of the United States, by which a part of its population is able to enjoy a life of extraordinary comfort and privilege, is not tenable over the long run as long as an enormous portion of the world lives in abject poverty, degradation and backwardness." – Mikhail Gorbachev, open letter to Bush and America, December 2000

"A taste of the ideas doing the rounds in Obama circles is offered by a recent report from the Managing Global Insecurity Project, whose small U.S. advisory group includes John Podesta, the man heading Mr. Obama's transition team and Strobe Talbott, the President of the Brookings Institution, from which Ms. Rice has just emerged. The MGI report agrees for the creation of a U.N. High Commissioner for counter-terrorism activity, a legally binding climate-change agreement negotiated under auspices of the U.N., and the creation of a 50,000 strong U.N. peacekeeping force. Once countries have pledged troops to this reserve army, the U.N. will have first call upon them." Financial Times, December 8, 2008, article "Now for a World Government"

President George Bush (Sr.) proclaimed the dawn of the "New World Order" when he was President. "New World Order" is written in Latin on the seal that overlooks the National Memorial in downtown Oklahoma City, among other places. Come see for yourself. The question is not IF there is a "new world order." The question is WHO will rule over it?

As just seen by your own eyes in the letter from Mikhail Gorbachev to American President George W. Bush in 2000, there is a battle for rulership over this new world empire we see culminating before our eyes.

The Bush faction believes they will rule over it. The Clinton faction thought they would, and still hopes to. But, I dare say that neither shall.

Posted in the Washington Post, June 7, 2009, Mikhail Gorbachev wrote an article titled, *"We Had Our Perestroika. It's High Time for Yours."*

Again, I encourage you to look it up and read it in its entirety. However, I find the following portion to be something to take great note of:

"The time has come for "creative construction," for striking the right balance between the government and the market, for integrating social and environmental factors and demilitarizing the economy. Washington will have to play a special role in this new perestroika, not just because the United States wields great economic, political and military power in today's global world, but because America was the main architect, and America's elite the main beneficiary, of the current world economic model. That model is now cracking and will, sooner or later, be replaced. That will be a complex and painful process for everyone, including the United States." – Mikhail Gorbachev, June 2009

I find a couple sentences in Gorbachev's latest article to stand out more than any other: *"That model is now cracking and will, sooner or later, be replaced. That will be a complex and painful process for everyone, including the United States."*

It will be very interesting to see what comes of America and the world stage during President Obama's administration. It is March 2010 at time of this last revision. "Obamacare" just passed the House vote and the fireworks are just getting started with all the federal lawsuits being filed by most of the States.

Let me go out on a limb here, and warn you not to look to America for your salvation. With G-d on our side, we can defend against all our enemies with a few rocks in our hands. However, without G-d on our side, all our great technology and military might will not protect us from the smallest of enemies. Saddam

Hussein was an evil man and Iraq was no match for the American military. But we should learn from history, with ancient Israel as our example. G-d will not be mocked, not even by the USA.

Look to Yeshua, the Messiah, to be your fortress and help in time of trouble. Wake up Believers! The days are evil. Why are you surprised at what is taking place?

These "co-conspirators," wherever they may be, are deceived individuals. They, like you and I, are easily deceived by the master of deception. That is why we must be on guard at all times. We must not let our pain overcome us.

Feel! Let yourself hurt. G-d gave us emotions. G-d has emotions. We are created in his image. Contrary to the teaching of evolutionists, we are the only creature created in G-d's image.

Incidentally, I heard a news report some years back about certain evolutionists proclaiming that man has stopped evolving. They say we have reached our potential and have arrived at the utopia for mankind. G-d laughs with amazement at such nonsense before he proclaims how foolish these people are.

"Wisdom calls aloud in the open air and raises her voice in the public places; she calls out at street corners and speaks out at entrances to city gates: 'How long, you whose lives have no purpose, will you love thoughtless living? How long will scorners find pleasure in mocking? How long will fools hate knowledge? Repent when I reprove -- I will pour out my spirit to you, I will make my words known to you. Because you refused when I called, and no one paid attention when I put out my hand, but instead you neglected my counsel and would not accept my reproof; I, in turn, will laugh at your distress, and mock when terror comes over you-- yes, when terror overtakes you like a storm and your disaster approaches like a whirlwind, when distress and trouble assail you, Then they will call me, but I won't answer; they will seek me earnestly, but they won't find me. Because they hated knowledge and did not choose the fear of ADONAI, they refused my counsel and despised my reproof. So they will bear the consequences of their own way and be overfilled with their own schemes. For the aimless wandering of the thoughtless will kill them, and the smug overconfidence of fools will destroy them; but those who pay attention to me will

live securely, untroubled by fear of misfortune.'"
(Mishlei/Proverbs 1:20-33)

Cry your heart out! It's ok to express yourself. But, let us not sin in our anger. Let us not allow the devil to trick us into believing that G-d is our enemy.

G-d is for us, who can be against us? We must hold fast to our faith even when we do not understand.

I encourage you to read the stories of the Bible. Read about the struggles that people like us had in times past. And don't read too fast. Try to see the big picture. What were the circumstances involved? What were the characters feeling at the time? Why would they say what they said or do what they did?

This brings us back to Saul and David. Both were kings of Israel. Both failed G-d many times. David murdered a man for his wife, whereas Saul murdered many out of paranoia and hatred. David fell into adultery and disobeyed G-d many times, but his rebellion was not like that of Saul's. Read for yourself.

In spite of David's shortcomings, G-d considered him a man after his own heart. What? A man after G-d's own heart committed adultery and murder? (Let us make a distinction between "falling into sin" and "practicing sin." The two are quite different and you can only grasp such an understanding when you study the scriptures in context and in their entirety.)

Again, step back and see the big picture.

What made David different from Saul?

Well, look at their responses to G-d's judgment upon them. They both suffered the consequences of their actions, but how did they deal with them?

Saul became bitter. He let jealousy and bitterness consume him. He gave Satan the foothold he desired in his life. He did not humble himself before G-d and admit the truth.

David, however, when confronted with the truth, did not hide from it. He acknowledged, confessed, and repented. He did not do penance, he repented.

T'SHUVA!

David did not make excuses or justify his sin and rewrite G-d's word to match his lifestyle. He confessed and repented.

T'SHUVA!

Are you still trying to "pay" for your sins? Be like David and let G-d cast them away. Get up, wipe yourself off, and "go and sin no more."

T'SHUVA!

This did not take away the consequences of his actions, nor the pain. But, it did restore him in proper standing with G-d and erased the power of sin and the enemy in his life.

"...G-d opposes the arrogant, but to the humble he gives grace. Therefore, submit to G-d. Moreover, take a stand against the Adversary, and he will flee from you. Come close to G-d, and he will come close to you. Clean your hands, sinners; and purify your hearts, you double minded people! Wail, mourn, sob! Let your laughter be turned into mourning and your joy into gloom. Humble yourselves before the Lord, and he will lift you up."
(Ya'akov/James 4:6-10)

T'SHUVA!

After just having his own firsthand experience learning about repentance and obedience, Yonah was sent by YHVH to warn the Non-Jewish city of Nineveh that they would be destroyed for their rebellion against G-d's Torah, or "rule of law."

"The word of ADONAI came to Yonah a second time: 'Set out for the great city of Ninveh, and proclaim to it the message I will give you.' So Yonah set out and went to Ninveh, as ADONAI had said. Now Ninveh was such a large city that it took three days just to cross it. Yonah began his entry into the city and had finished only his first day of proclaiming, 'In forty days Ninveh will be overthrown,' when the people of Ninveh believed G-d.

"They proclaimed a fast and put on sackcloth, from the greatest of them to the least. When the news reached the king of Ninveh, he got up from his throne, took off his robe, put on sackcloth and sat in ashes. He then had this proclamation made throughout Ninveh:

"'By decree of the King and his nobles, no person or animal, herd or flock, is to put anything in his mouth; they are neither to eat nor drink water. They must be covered with sackcloth, both people and animals, and they are to cry out to G-d with all their might -- let each of them turn from his evil way and from the violence they practice. Who knows? Maybe G-d will change his mind, relent and turn from his fierce anger; and then we won't perish.'

"When G-d saw by their deeds that they had turned from their evil way, he relented and did not bring on them the punishment he had threatened." (Yonah/Jonah 3:1-10)

Let us look at some examples of T'shuva from G-d's perspective. Pay close attention to many of these. They speak of more than just t'shuva, they prophecy of the very days we now live. To him who has ears to hear, listen to what the Spirit says:

*"In your distress, when all these things have come upon you, in the acharit-hayamim, you will **return** to ADONAI your G-d and listen to what he says; for ADONAI your G-d is a merciful G-d. He will not fail you, destroy you, or forget the covenant with your ancestors which he swore to them." (D'varim/Deuteronomy 4:30, 31)*

*"When the time arrives that all these things have come upon you, both the blessing and the curse which I have presented to you; and you are there among the nations to which ADONAI your G-d has driven you; then, at last, you will start thinking about what has happened to you and you will **return** to ADONAI your G-d and pay attention to what he has said, which will be exactly what I am ordering you to do today -- you and your children, with all your heart and all your being. **At that point, ADONAI your G-d will reverse your exile and show you mercy; he will return and gather you from all the peoples to which ADONAI your G-d scattered you.** If one of yours was scattered to the far end of the sky, ADONAI your G-d will gather you even from there; he will go there and get you. ADONAI your G-d will bring you back into the land your ancestors possessed, and you will possess it; he will make you prosper there, and you will become even more numerous than your ancestors. Then ADONAI your G-d will circumcise your hearts and the hearts of your children, so that you will love ADONAI your G-d with all your heart and all your being, and thus you will live. ADONAI your G-d will put all these curses on your enemies, on those who hated and persecuted you; but you will **return** and pay attention to what ADONAI says and obey all his mitzvot which I am giving you today....For this mitzvah which I am giving you today is not too hard for you, it is not beyond your reach. It isn't in the sky, so that you need to ask, 'Who will go up into the sky for us, bring it to us and make us hear it, so that we can obey it:' Likewise, it isn't beyond the sea, so that you need to ask, 'Who will cross the sea for us, bring it to us and make us hear it, so that we can obey it?' On the contrary, the word is very close to you -- in your mouth, even in your heart; therefore, you can do it!" (D'varim/Deuteronomy 30:1-14)*

*"If I shut up the sky, so that there is no rain; or if I order locusts to devour the land; or if I send an epidemic of sickness among my people; then, if my people, who bear my name, will humble themselves, pray, seek my face and **turn** from their evil ways, I will hear from heaven, forgive their sin and heal their land." (Divrei-Hayamim Alef/2 Chronicles 7:13, 14)*

Has America turned from her sins? Hardly. United States Rep. (now Senator) Lindsey Graham (SC), you and your colleagues are too easily impressed with your singing. (This comment is reference to his excitement over the Congressmen and women singing together on the steps of Congress after 9/11 and to the "Day of Prayer and Remembrance.")

A better term for that "Day of Prayer" is a "Day of Blaspheme." G-d is not impressed with words, and he is definitely not pleased by a nation that prays to Him and Allah in the same breath. That is idolatry!

*"All the ends of the earth will remember and **turn** to ADONAI; all the clans of the nations will worship in your presence. **For the kingdom belongs to ADONAI, and he rules the nations.**" (Tehillim/Psalms 22:27, 28)*

*"I know, ADONAI, that your rulings are righteous, that even when you humble me you are faithful. Let your grace comfort me, in keeping with your promise to your servant. Show me pity, and I will live, for your Torah is my delight. Let the proud be ashamed, because they wrong me with lies; as for me, I will meditate on your precepts. Let those who fear you **turn** to me, along with those who know your instruction. Let my heart be pure in your laws, so that I won't be put to shame." (Tehillim/Psalms 119: 75-80)*

*"**Repent** when I reprove -- I will pour out my spirit to you, I will make my words known to you." (Mishlei/Proverbs 1:23)*

*"Like hovering birds, ADONAI-Tzva'ot will protect Yerushalayim. In protecting it, he will rescue it; in sparing it, he will save it. People of Isra'el! **Return** to him to whom you have been so deeply disloyal!" (Yesha'yahu/Isaiah 31:5, 6)*

*"'Isra'el, if you will **return**,' says ADONAI, 'yes, **return** to me; and if you will banish your abominations from my presence without wandering astray again; and if you will swear, 'As*

ADONAI lives,' in truth, justice and righteousness; then the nations will bless themselves by him, and in him will they glory." (Yirmeyahu/Jeremiah 4:1, 2)

"At one time, I may speak about uprooting, breaking down and destroying a nation or kingdom; but if that nation turns from their evil, which prompted me to speak against it, then I relent concerning the disaster I had planned to inflict on it. Similarly, at another time, I may speak about building and planting a nation or kingdom; but if it behaves wickedly from my perspective and doesn't listen to what I say, then I change my mind and don't do the good I said I would do that would have helped it." (Yirmeyahu/Jeremiah 18:7-10)

*"Maybe they will listen, and each of them **turn** from his evil way; then I will be able to relent from the disaster I intend to bring on them because of how evil their deeds are." (Yirmeyahu/Jeremiah 26:3)*

"I will gather them out of all the countries where I drove them in my anger, fury and great wrath; and I will bring them back to this place and have them live here in safety. They will be my people, and I will be their G-d. I will give them singleness of heart and singleness of purpose, so that they will fear me forever -- this will be for their own good and for the good of their children after them. I will make with them an everlasting covenant not to turn away from them, but to do them good; I will put fear of me in their hearts, so that they will not leave me." (Yirmeyahu/Jeremiah 32:37-40)

"Who can say something and have it happen without ADONAI'S commanding it? Don't both bad things and good proceed from the mouth of the Most High? Why should anyone alive complain, even a strong man, about the punishment for his sins? Let us examine and test our ways and return to ADONAI. Let us lift up our hearts and our hands to G-d in heaven and say, 'We, for our part, have transgressed and rebelled; you, for your part, have not forgotten.'" (Eikhah/Lamentations 3:37-42)

*"Do I take any pleasure at all in having the wicked person die?' asks ADONAI Elohim. 'Wouldn't I prefer that he **turn** from his ways and live? On the other hand, when the righteous person*

*turns away from his righteousness and commits wickedness by acting in accordance with all the disgusting practices that the wicked person does, will he live? None of the righteous deeds he has done will be remembered; for the trespasses and sins he has committed, he will die. So now you say, 'ADONAI'S way isn't fair.' Listen, house of Isra'el! Is it my way that is unfair? or your ways that are unfair? When the righteous person turns away from his righteousness and commits wickedness, he will die for it -- for the wickedness he commits he will die. And when the wicked person **turns** away from all the wickedness he has committed and does what is lawful and right, he will save his life. Because he thinks it over and **repents** of all the transgressions he committed, he will certainly live, not die. Yet the house of Isra'el says, 'ADONAI'S way isn't fair.' House of Isra'el, is it my ways that are unfair, or your ways that are unfair? Therefore, house of Isra'el, I will judge each of you according to his ways,' says ADONAI Elohim. '**Repent**, and turn yourselves away from all your transgressions, so that they will not be a stumbling block that brings guilt upon you. Throw far away from yourselves all your crimes that you committed, and make yourselves a new heart and a new spirit; for why should you die, house of Isra'el? I take no pleasure in the death of anyone who dies,' says ADONAI Elohim,' so **turn** yourselves around and live!"* (Yechezk'el/Ezekiel 18:23-32)

"Yet even now,' says ADONAI, 'turn to me with all your heart, with fasting, weeping and lamenting.' Tear your heart, not your garments; and turn to ADONAI your G-d. For he is merciful and compassionate, slow to anger, rich in grace, and willing to change his mind about disaster. Who knows? He may turn, change his mind and leave a blessing behind him..." (Yo'el/Joel 2:12-14)

Now, having seen what T'shuva, repentance, is from G-d's perspective, can you say that you and your nation have truly repented of your sins and turned to the Living G-d? Can England claim true T'shuva? Can Ethiopia claim true T'shuva? Can South Africa claim true T'shuva? Can Japan? Korea? Saudi Arabia? Iraq? China? Russia? Can Israel or the United States of America claim to truly have repented of their sins?

You be the judge yourself. Since 9/11, have you seen a change in any of our nations' sins? Oh sure, "G-d bless America" is plastered all over the place and the song is sung at most public gatherings since then. A national Day of Remembrance was called and other gatherings since then. But, can we honestly say that America has repented? Can Israel claim to have done T'shuva? Sure G-d's promises are true, but Israel still remains 2/3 secular and many who are religious are dead within their hearts.

(Watch and be awed as you see the Spirit be restored to the flesh and bones that YHVH has brought back to the land he promised his friend Avraham, as was prophesied by Yechezk'el, aka Ezekiel.)

I was thoroughly impressed by the opening ceremonies of the 2002 Winter Olympics in Salt Lake City. It was one of the best I've ever seen. It was very inspiring as an American. On the surface, President George W. Bush is my kind of President. BUT...

Has abortion ceased? Has divorce decreased? Has pornography been taken off the counters and removed from the internet? Has prayer and the scriptures been allowed back into schools? Has the ACLU ceased its fight against the G-d of Israel and put their faith in Yeshua? Is homosexuality called the perversion that it is, or are lawmakers seeking to protect it and criminalize those who preach G-d's word against such evil? Have the commandments of G-d been proclaimed to be truth and the nation's standards for righteousness?

NEAH! Nothing has changed! On the contrary, prime time television has gone on with its more risqué and vulgar programming. G-d is still a generic god and any specific name of G-d, other than Allah, is not allowed to be proclaimed or prayed to publicly. The 10 Commandments of YHVH are banned from schools while the 5 pillars of Islam are touted and taught with pride. Jesus is a banned "cuss word," while Allah is praised!

The killing of millions of innocent children in the womb is not even wept over, but rather is unconstitutionally funded by taxpayer money. Divorce is still winced at and ministers even stay in the pulpit after leaving their wives. Allah is given preeminence, while Yeshua is banned from even the basement.

I could go on with more, but I believe G-d's word is clear. If you can't see it after reading this far, then what hope do you have?

To shed light on G-d's grace towards nations, let us remember the example Israel serves to the world. It is very clear that Israel is not cast away. We Gentile believers have been grafted in. If Israel is cast away, then so are we. For Paul, the apostle to the Gentiles, the one the "Church Universal" quotes the most and holds in high regard, even he speaks against this very teaching.

"In that case, I say, isn't it that they have stumbled with the result that they have permanently fallen away?" Heaven forbid! Quite the contrary, it is by means of their stumbling that the deliverance has come to the Gentiles, in order to provoke them to jealousy. Moreover, if their stumbling is bringing riches to the world -- that is, if Israel's being placed TEMPORARILY (capitals mine) *in a condition less favored than that of the Gentiles is bringing riches to the latter -- HOW MUCH GREATER RICHES WILL ISRAEL IN ITS FULLNESS BRING THEM!*

*"However, **to those of you who are Gentiles** I say this: since I myself am an emissary sent to the Gentiles, I make known the importance of my work in the hope that somehow I may provoke some of my own people to jealousy and save some of them! For if their casting Yeshua aside means reconciliation for the world, what will their accepting him mean? It will be life from the dead!*

*"Now if the hallah offered as firstfuits is holy, so is the whole loaf. And if the root is holy, so are the branches. But if some of the branches were broken off, and you -- a wild olive -- were grafted in among them and have become equal sharers in the rich root of the olive tree, then don't boast, **remember that you are not supporting the root, the root is supporting you.** So you will say, 'Branches were broken off so that I might be grafted in.' True, but so what? They were broken off because of their lack of trust. However, you keep your place only because of your trust.*

*"**SO DON'T BE ARROGANT; ON THE CONTRARY, BE TERRIFIED!*** (capitals mine)

"For if G-d did not spare the natural branches, he certainly won't spare you! So take a good look at G-d's kindness and his severity: on the one hand, severity toward those who fell off; but, on the other hand, G-d's kindness toward you --- provided you maintain yourself in that kindness! **OTHER WISE, YOU TOO WILL BE CUT OFF!** *Moreover, the others, if they do not persist in their lack of trust, will be grafted in: because* **G-D IS ABLE TO GRAFT THEM BACK IN.** *For if you were cut out of what is by nature a wild olive tree and grafted, contrary to nature, into a cultivated olive tree, how much more will these natural branches be grafted back into their own olive tree!*

"For, brothers, I want you to understand this truth which G-d formerly concealed but has now revealed, so that you won't imagine you know more than you actually do. It is that stoniness, to a degree, has come upon Isra'el, **UNTIL THE GENTILE WORLD ENTERS IN ITS FULLNESS***; and that it is in this way that all Isra'el will be saved. As the Tanakh says,*

"Out of Tziyon will come the Redeemer; he will turn away ungodliness from Ya'akov and this will be my covenant with them... when I take away their sins." *(Romans 11:11-27)*

HISTORY LESSON:

Question: How long has Israel been in exile?

Answer: From the final Diaspora in 70 A.C.E. to 1948 A.C.E. when she was "reborn" as a nation with Jerusalem being restored to her hands in 1967!

Did you notice something? **ISRAEL'S EXILE HAS CEASED!!!**

Israel has come out of captivity and returned to the land that YHVH had promised his friend Avraham (Abraham), through Yitz'chak (Isaac) and Ya'akov (Jacob).

Listen to G-d people! Stop listening to the preachers who teach falsehood and lies about the days we live in. Hear it from G-d himself:

"Now you, human being, prophesy to the mountains of Isra'el. Say: 'Mountains of Isra'el, hear the message from ADONAI. ADONAI Elohim says: 'The enemy is boasting over you, 'Ha! Even the ancient high places are ours now!' Therefore prophecy, and say that ADONAI Elohim says, 'Because they

desolated you and swallowed you up from every side, so that the other nations could take possession of you; and now people are gossiping about you and slandering you; therefore, mountains of Isra'el, hear the message of ADONAI Elohim -- this is what ADONAI Elohim says to the mountains and hills, the streams and valleys, the desolate wastes and the abandoned cities, now preyed on and derided by the other surrounding nations -- therefore this is what ADONAI Elohim says;

"In the heat of my jealousy I speak against the other nations and all of Edom, since, rejoicing with all their heart, they have arrogated my land to themselves as a possession and, with utter contempt, seized it as prey.

"Therefore prophesy concerning the land of Isra'el, and say to the mountains, the hills, the streams and the valleys that ADONAI Elohim says this: 'I speak in my jealousy and fury, because you have endured being shamed by the nations. Therefore thus says ADONAI Elohim: 'I have raised my hand and sworn that the nations surrounding you will bear their shame. But you, mountains of Isra'el, you will sprout your branches and bear your fruit for my people Isra'el, who will soon return.

"I am here for you, and I will turn toward you; then you will be tilled and sown; and I will multiply your population, all the house of Isra'el, all of it. The cities will be inhabited and the ruins rebuilt. I will multiply both the human and animal populations, they will increase and be productive; and I will cause you to be inhabited as you were before -- indeed, I will do you more good than before; and you will know that I am ADONAI. I will cause people to walk on you, my people Isra'el; they will possess you, and you will be their inheritance; never again will you make them childless.'

"ADONAI Elohim says, 'Because they say to you, 'Land, you devour people and make your nations childless,' therefore you will no longer devour people, and you will not make your nations childless anymore,' says ADONAI Elohim. 'I will not permit the nations to shame you, or the peoples to reproach you any longer; and you will no more cause your nations to stumble,' says ADONAI Elohim.

"The word of the Lord came to me: 'Human being, when the house of Isra'el lived in their own land, they defiled it by their manner of life and their actions; their way before me was like the uncleanness of niddah. Therefore I poured out my fury on them, because of the blood they had shed in the land and because they defiled it with their idols. I scattered them among the nations and dispersed them throughout the countries; I judged them in keeping with their manner of life and actions. When they came to the nations they were going to, they profaned my holy name; so that people said of them, 'These are ADONAI'S people, who have been exiled from his land.' But I am concerned about my holy name, which the house of Isra'el is profaning among the nations where they have gone.

"Therefore tell the house of Isra'el that ADONAI Elohim says this: **'I AM NOT GOING TO DO THIS FOR YOUR SAKE, HOUSE OF ISRA'EL, BUT FOR THE SAKE OF MY HOLY NAME, WHICH YOU HAVE BEEN PROFANING AMONG THE NATIONS WHERE YOU WENT.** *I will set apart my great name to be regarded as holy, since it has been profaned in the nations -- you profaned it among them.* **THE NATIONS WILL KNOW THAT I AM ADONAI,**' *says ADONAI Elohim, 'when, before their eyes, I am set apart through you to be regarded as holy,*

" **FOR I WILL TAKE YOU FROM AMONG THE NATIONS, GATHER YOU FROM ALL THE COUNTRIES, AND RETURN YOU TO YOU OWN SOIL. THEN I WILL SPRINKLE CLEAN WATER ON YOU, AND YOU WILL BE CLEAN;** *I will cleanse you from all your uncleanness and from all your idols. I will give you a new heart and put a new spirit inside you; I will take the stony heart out of your flesh and give you a heart of flesh. I will put my Spirit inside you and cause you to live by my laws, respect my rulings and obey them.*

" **YOU WILL LIVE IN THE LAND I GAVE TO YOUR ANCESTORS.** *You will be my people, and I will be your G-d. I will save you from all your uncleanliness. I will summon the grain and increase it, and not send famine against you. I will multiply the yield of fruit from the trees and increase production in the fields, so that you never again suffer the reproach of*

famine among the nations. **Then you will remember your evil ways and your actions that were not good; as you look at yourselves, you will loathe yourselves for your guilt and disgusting practices. UNDERSTAND,' SAYS ADONAI ELOHIM, 'THAT I AM NOT DOING THIS FOR YOUR SAKE. Instead, be ashamed and dismayed for your ways, house of Isra'el."** *(Yechezk'el/Ezekiel 36:1-32)*

He who has ears to hear, let him hear.

WHAT'S THE PURPOSE?

"The crime which bankrupts men and nations is that of turning aside from one's main purpose to serve a job here and there." - Ralph Waldo Emerson

I don't claim to know Mr. Emerson's religious beliefs, but his comment is something worth taking note of.

So, what's your purpose in life? I suppose if you have made it this far that you are either very curious or a seeker after righteousness. I hope you are the latter.

For you who fear YHVH, it is not fit for me to call you to repentance and leave you without words of encouragement. It is my desire to spur you on and encourage you. For the coming days will not be easy. You may find yourself in circumstances that will test your faith in ways you never imagined.

Therefore, I implore you to read G-d's word while you are still free to do so. Study it while you can. Eat it and let it become a part of you. Pray and seek the Lord while he can be found, for soon the days of trouble will become great. Do not be discouraged or dismayed. BE STRONG AND COURAGEOUS, FOR THE LORD YOUR G-D IS WITH YOU!

Remember our Messiah's words:

"But when they bring you to trial, do not worry about what to say or how to say it; when the time comes, you will be given what you should say. For it will not be just you speaking, but the Spirit of your heavenly Father speaking through you.

"A brother will betray his brother to death, and a father his child; children will turn against their parents and have them put to death. Everyone will hate you because of me, but whoever holds out till the end will be preserved from harm. When you are persecuted in one town, run away to another. Yes indeed; I tell you, you will not finish going through the towns of Isra'el before the Son of Man comes.

"A talmid is not greater than his rabbi, a slave is not greater than his master. It is enough for a talmid that he become like his rabbi, and a slave like his master. Now if people have called the head of the house Ba'al-Zibbul, how much more will they malign the members of his household! So do not fear them; for there is nothing covered that will not be uncovered, or hidden that will not be known. What I tell you in the dark, speak in the light; what is whispered in your ear, proclaim on the housetops.

"Do not fear those who kill the body but are powerless to kill the soul. Rather, fear him who can destroy both soul and body in Gei-Hinnom. Aren't sparrows sold for next to nothing, two for an assarion? Yet not one of them will fall to the ground without your Father's consent. As for you, every hair on your head has been counted. So do not be afraid, you are worth more than many sparrows.

"Whoever acknowledges me in the presence of others I will also acknowledge in the presence of my Father in heaven. But whoever disowns me before others I will disown before my Father in heaven. Don't suppose that I have come to bring peace to the Land. It is not peace I have come to bring, but a sword!

"For I have come to set a man against his father, a daughter against her mother, a daughter-in-law against her mother-in-law, so that a man's enemies will be the members of his own household.

"Whoever loves his father or mother more than he loves me is not worthy of me; anyone who loves his son or daughter more than he loves me is not worthy of me. And anyone who does not take up his execution-stake and follow me is not worthy of me.

"Whoever finds his own life will lose it, but the person who loses his life for my sake will find it. Whoever receives you is receiving me, and whoever receives me is receiving the One who sent me. Anyone who receives a prophet because he is a prophet will receive the reward a prophet gets, and anyone who receives a tzaddik because he is a tzaddik will receive the reward a tzaddik gets. Indeed, if anyone gives just a cup of cold water to one of these little ones because he is my talmid -- yes! -- I tell you, he will certainly not lose his reward!" (Mattityahu/Matthew 10:19-42)

What's the purpose of life?

Before I answer that question, I want you to take a deep breath. Take a couple deep breaths for a moment.

Take a few seconds and look around you. What do you see? Who do you see?

Maybe things are really buzzing around you. Or maybe you're in the country and all is calm and quiet. It doesn't matter.

Have you ever heard the saying, "It won't matter a hundred years from now"? Depending on the point trying to be made, I would usually agree with this philosophy. However, for this discussion, this saying would be untrue.

It will matter in a hundred years from now! What? What will matter in a hundred years?

You and what you do will matter in a hundred years from now.

"Me?" you ask. Yes, you.

Ever see "It's a Wonderful Life" with Jimmy Stewart? I'm sure that those born before the 1980's have seen it more than they care. It used to, and still does in places, come on television during the Christmas holidays. I remember one year, it was probably on every night for a couple weeks on different cable channels. Talk about over doing it. Some people can't stand it anymore because of its over showing. But, that's beside the point.

The point? Ahh, yes. The point is, that no matter what you think of the movie, (with its erroneous teaching about angels), it's a good show about how you and I impact this world. Even when we feel like we don't have anything to contribute to it, or like Stewart's character, think we have something else to contribute than that which we are.

What do you have to contribute? Isn't that another way to look at it? Contribution! Isn't that really what we want out of life?

What's my purpose in life? What can I contribute to the overall scheme of things? What is my contribution to life?

I want to make a contribution....a contribution to G-d's creation, to G-d's work, to G-d's Kingdom!

Believe it or not, this came to me while I was having my own pity party and feeling like my life was so worthless and empty. Yes, I was.

Do you really think that you are the only one who still has questions about your own existence? Well, you're not. That's one of the reasons why I'm writing this book. To let you know that you're not alone! Everyone around you struggles from time to time with "self-validation."

Even the great prophet Eliyahu (Elijah), a man like you and me, struggled with depression and his trust in G-d. M'lakhim Alef (1 Kings) 18 & 19 tells us how he called down fire from heaven and killed the prophets of Ba'al. Then he went into the mountains to hide for his life and even prayed for G-d to kill him.

"Validation? I thought you were going to say self-esteem."

Self-esteem. To esteem is to regard or admire.

To self-admire? When we look in the mirror, can we honestly say that we admire what or who we see? If you do admire yourself, (void of Messiah, just looking at the person in the mirror), then obviously this book isn't for you. Humanism is your religion. You are reading the wrong book. Sorry to bother you. Go please yourself while the rest of us seek after G-d's peace that passes understanding.

Is self-admiration what our children really need? Is that what you and I need? What our children, you, and I need is... "validation," by G-d AND self.

To validate: (according to the American Heritage Dictionary) to declare or make legally valid; to mark with an indication of official sanction; to substantiate or verify.

Validity: the state or quality of being valid.

Are you valid? Or are you a mistake?

According to G-d you are not a mistake. You are valid! When you become a new creation in Messiah, G-d validates you completely.

So, what's with "self-validation"?

To self-validate: (according to this author) to accept your valid state of being as G-d has declared it. Quit walking around like a defeated Eagle and accept the Great Eagle's declaration of who you are in him.

Notice that it is AS G-D HAS DECLARED! Not as you, the government, your moma or daddy, or the Devil has declared, but as G-d has declared.

This is the battle of the universe. John 3:14-21. If we reject Messiah and stand on our own goodness, we self-validate the wrong way, thus being invalid. If we walk in self-pity instead of victory, we may be G-d-validated, but our self has invalidated G-d's truth about us and, therefore, calls Yeshua a liar. When our self accepts Messiah's atonement AND transformation of our beings, we reach true "self-validation." That's how I like to put it. The professionals and pundits can bicker with me all they want, but who's writing this book anyway? So that's "self-validation" according to me. Thank you for your understanding. (smile)

Don't build a new doctrine on this word, just understand my point. The purpose of life is to reach self-validation and help others reach self-validation. What does that mean? It means receiving and sharing the Gospel.

ACCEPTING AND SHARING THE GOOD NEWS OF YESHUA, THE MESSIAH, IS THE PURPOSE OF LIFE!

To be changed from a Turkey to an Eagle, if you will. And to see yourself as the Eagle G-d has transformed you into. And to help others be "born again" as a new creation in Messiah as you have.

"Brothers, my heart's deepest desire and my prayer to G-d for Isra'el is for their salvation; for I can testify to their zeal for G-d. But it is not based on correct understanding; for, since they are unaware of G-d's way of making people righteous and instead seek to set up their own, they have not submitted themselves to G-d's way of making people righteous. For the goal at which the Torah aims is the Messiah, who offers righteousness to everyone who trusts. For Moshe writes about the righteousness grounded in the Torah that the person who does these things will attain life through them. Moreover, the righteousness grounded in trusting says: "Do not say in your heart, 'Who will ascend to heaven?'"--that is to bring the Messiah down--or, '"Who will descend into Sh'ol?"'-- that is to bring the Messiah up from the dead. What, then, does it say?

"The word is near you, in your mouth and in your heart."--that is, the word about trust which we proclaim, namely,

"that if you acknowledge publicly with your mouth that Yeshua is Lord and trust in your heart that G-d raised him from the dead, you will be delivered. For with the heart one goes on trusting and thus continues toward righteousness, while with the mouth one keeps on making public acknowledgment and thus continues toward deliverance.

"For the passage quoted says that everyone who rests his trust on him will not be humiliated. That means that there is no difference between Jew and Gentile--ADONAI is the same for everyone, rich toward everyone who calls on him, since everyone who calls on the name of ADONAI will be delivered.

"But how can they call on someone if they haven't trusted in him? And how can they trust in someone if they haven't heard about him? And how can they hear about someone if no one is proclaiming him? And how can people proclaim him unless G-d sends them?--as the Tanakh puts it, "How beautiful are the feet of those announcing good news about good things!" (Romans 10:1-15)

"Is that all?" In a nutshell, Yes.

The bottom line is yes, that is it. But, as we humans are, we cannot live with this simplistic answer. It's too easy!

So, here is a detailed and longer version of self-validation. Remember, this is GRACE "Old Covenant" style:

"G-d, in your grace, have mercy on me; in your great compassion, blot out my crimes. Wash me completely from my guilt, and cleanse me from my sin. For I know my crimes, my sin confronts me all the time.

"Against you, you only, have I sinned and done what is evil from your perspective; so that you are right in accusing me and justified in passing sentence. True, I was born guilty, was a sinner from the moment my mother conceived me. Still, you want truth in the inner person; so make me know wisdom in my inmost heart.

"Sprinkle me with oregano, and I shall be clean; wash me, and I will be whiter than snow. Let me hear the sound of joy and

gladness, so that the bones you crushed can rejoice. Turn away your face from my sins, and blot out all my crimes.

"Create in me a clean heart, G-d; renew in me a resolute spirit. Don't thrust me away from your presence, and don't take your Ruach Kodesh away from me. Restore my joy in your salvation, and let a willing spirit uphold me.

"THEN I will teach the wicked your ways, and sinners will return to you. Rescue me from the guilt of shedding blood, G-d, G-d of my salvation! Then my tongue will sing about your righteousness -- ADONAI, open my lips; then my mouth will praise you.

"For you don't want sacrifices, or I would give them; you don't take pleasure in burnt offerings. My sacrifice to G-d is a broken spirit; G-d, you won't spurn a broken, chastened heart

"In your good pleasure, make Tziyon prosper; rebuild the walls of Yerushalayim. Then you will delight in righteous sacrifices, in burnt offerings and whole burnt offerings; then they will offer bulls on your altar." (Tehillim/Psalms 51)

Tell me again that grace is only for the "New Covenant". King David, along with many others, disagrees with you.

"I will bless ADONAI at all times; his praise will always be in my mouth. When I boast, it will be about you; the humble will hear of it and be glad.

"Proclaim with me the greatness of ADONAI; and let us exalt his name together. I sought ADONAI, and he answered me; he rescued me from everything I feared.

"They looked to him and grew radiant; their faces will never blush for shame. This poor man cried; ADONAI heard and saved him from all his troubles. The angel of ADONAI, who encamps around those who fear him, delivers them.

"Taste, and see that ADONAI is good. How blessed are those who take refuge in him! Fear ADONAI, you holy ones of his, for those who fear him lack nothing.

"Young lions can be needy, they can go hungry, but those who seek ADONAI lack nothing good. Come, children, listen to me; I will teach you the fear of ADONAI.

"Which of you takes pleasure in living? Who wants a long life to see good things? Keep your tongue from evil and your lips *from deceiving talk; turn from evil, and do good; seek peace, go after it! The eyes of ADONAI watch over the righteous, and his ears are open to their cry. But the face of ADONAI opposes those who do evil, to cut off all memory of them from the earth.*

"They cried out, and ADONAI heard, and he saved them from all their troubles. ADONAI is near those with broken hearts; he saves those whose spirit is crushed.

"The righteous person suffers many evils, but ADONAI rescues him out of them all. He protects all his bones; not one of them gets broken.

"Evil will kill the wicked, and those who hate the righteous will be condemned. But ADONAI redeems his servants; and no one who takes refuge in him will be condemned." (Tehillim/Psalm 34)

Do you still believe the Old Covenant is without Grace? You must not be reading it then. It is full of Grace. What are Yom Kippur and Pesach all about? Just as G-d's grace abounded throughout "Old Covenant" times, so does his law still stand in the "New Covenant" times. The two are not exclusive of one another. On the contrary, they are one and the same. How can you understand if you only listen to the fools who claim to know more than you as they hold up their Seminary degrees?

"My son, don't forget my teaching, KEEP MY COMMANDS IN YOUR HEART; for they will add to you many days, years of life and peace. DO NOT LET GRACE AND TRUTH LEAVE YOU -- bind them around your neck; WRITE THEM ON THE TABLET OF YOUR HEART

(Which is it? G-d's law or G-d's grace on our hearts? Oh, there must be a connection then. Looks like BOTH. Don't you agree?)

"Then you will win favor and esteem in the sight of G-d and of people. Trust in ADONAI with all your heart; do not rely on your own understanding. In all your ways acknowledge him; then he will level your paths. Don't be conceited about your own wisdom; but fear ADONAI, and turn from evil. This will bring health to your body and give strength to your bones. Honor ADONAI with your wealth and with the firstfruits of all your income. Then your granaries will be filled and your vats overflow

with new wine. My son, don't despise ADONAI'S discipline or resent his reproof; for ADONAI corrects those he loves like a father who delights in his son." (Mishlei/Proverbs 3:1-12)

I could continue with more, but it has already been written. So, I refer you to the Old Covenant and New Covenant writings, commonly referred to as the Bible, for more.

Back to earlier...Take another breath. What/who did you see earlier? What/who did you hear?

You need air to breath, right? You need food and water to live, right? You need a job to pay for the necessities of life, right? You need love to make it all worthwhile too, right? Otherwise, we are back at the beginning. What's the purpose? Right?

From a strictly physical and secular perspective, we work for a living. All our lives are spent preparing for the next day. We feed ourselves to give ourselves the energy to get through the day so that we can get on to the next. Every day: eat, drink, work, eat, drink, play (if not more work), rest, eat, drink, bathe (hopefully), sleep. And the next day all over again.

Of course not everyone has the same job or activities in a day, but the basics are there for everyone. Eat, drink, work, sleep. And then we die on the last day.

Morbid? That's not morbid. You see, we've lost perspective of this life. Death is a part of life. Sounds strange, doesn't it. But, contrary to the media's fascination with life eternal on earth, death is natural. It happens eventually. It's inevitable! So, let's stop kidding ourselves and admit our mortality.

Isn't it interesting to note that death, according to Luke, is considered an "exodus"? Look at what he said,

*"About a week after Yeshua said these things, he took Kefa, Yochanan and Ya'akov with him and went up to the hill country to pray. As he was praying, the appearance of his face changed; and his clothing became gleaming white. Suddenly there were two men talking with him--Moshe and Eliyahu! They appeared in glorious splendor and spoke of his **exodus**, which he was soon to accomplish in Yerushalayim." (Luke 9:28-31)*

What exodus? His death on the tree was to be his exodus. Is death to be feared? Not for those who die in Messiah. Why then do you fear the inevitable?

We are not immortal! We are mortal!

"Make me grasp, ADONAI, what my end must be, what it means that my days are numbered; let me know what a transient creature I am. You have made my days like handbreadths; for you, the length of my life is like nothing. Yes, everyone, no matter how firmly he stands, is merely a puff of wind. Humans go about like shadows; their turmoil is all for nothing. They accumulate wealth, not knowing who will enjoy its benefits." (Tehillim/Psalms 39:4-7)

"Look, I will tell you a secret -- not all of us will die! But we will all be changed! It will take but a moment, the blink of an eye, at the final shofar. For the shofar will sound, and the dead will be raised to live forever, and we too will be changed. For this material which can decay must be clothed with imperishability, this which is mortal must be clothed with immortality. When what decays puts on imperishability and what is mortal puts on immortality, then this passage in the Tanakh will be fulfilled:

"Death is swallowed up in victory. Death, where is your victory? Death, where is your sting?" (I Corinthians. 15:51-55)

The human mind is always trying to prolong life. We all are trying to prolong our lives. We really don't want to die. We try not to think about it. We do a pretty good job about denying the existence of death until someone we know "gets their pink slip."

Then, we can't help but acknowledge it...for a while. Then, we get back to "living" again, and "denying" that life, our life, will cease someday.

By the way, suicide is not an option. Suicide is not faith. Suicide is unbelief. For a soldier to go on a "suicide" mission to fight for freedom (with the hopes of surviving and returning home, but knowing that death is most probable, as opposed to strapping explosives around oneself to kill self and innocent civilians) is not the same as a poor fool who has lost all hope and decides to reject life in Yeshua and end his life by suicide. Do not let the Devil deceive you! The Living Water is yours for the taking. Put your faith and trust in him and serve him until he calls you home. Don't abort your mission. Fight until the end.

Yes, sooner or later, you and I will say goodbye to this world and sleep with our ancestors until the resurrection at Messiah's second coming.

Soap box time!

It amazes me that scientists, the media, and politicians are so fascinated with "saving lives" through cloning and stem cell research. Let me be frank here folks, YOU AREN'T "SAVING" ANYONE'S LIFE!!!

You may extend it for a bit longer, but all you will be able to do is put off the inevitable, DEATH.

What? Is G-d not able to heal our diseases? Is he not able to provide our sustenance? Is the creation he made not good enough for you that you have to mutate it into what you think is better?

When G-d created all of creation, in six days by the way, he said it was GOOD. Then why do we try to change it and make it better? Have we succeeded in making anything truly better than the way G-d created it? We've discovered vast resources and put them to good use, but do we improve on anything when we mess with the genetic code that G-d wrote?

Sin and disobedience = curse: drought, famine, AIDS and other diseases, natural disasters ("global warming"), sick fruits and veggies, wimpy livestock, death, and destruction.

Trust and obedience to Yeshua = blessing: rain, plenty, healing, peace and tranquility in nature, healthy fruits and veggies, large healthy livestock, long life, and productivity.

To you law makers and politicians, who think singing a song or saying a prayer is good enough, I say to you, "You are a form of godliness, denying the power thereof. Without trusting and obeying Yeshua, there is no hope in anything you do." G-d will not bless you, because you do not bless him and give him the praise due his Holy Name.

Why are you so afraid to die, O man? What is it that you fear? Why is it so hard to trust in G-d for your health and well-being? Is he not able to feed the sparrow or clothe the lillies? Why then do you refuse to acknowledge your Creator and cry to him for your deliverance?

Dolly, the cloned sheep, got arthritis! Mad cow and foot & mouth disease hit England shortly after that great cloning "success" of science. Do you think G-d is trying to say something to you mockers of G-d and perverters of his creation?

Massive snow storms, multiple tornadoes for multiple days, 500 year floods (plural) all around the world, earthquakes more often and more powerful than ever in recorded history, unusual weather, unusual world events..... But, it's just global warming, right? No, it's birth pains! And they will increase in number and in magnitude!

If the Holy Scriptures, being inspired by G-d through Moses and the prophets, are true, then why do you scoff? If such events have nothing to do with the sins of nations, then why do you even pay lip-service to G-d and his word? If it's all just a bunch of myths and superstitions, why do you cry to G-d for help when disaster strikes? Is singing "G-d Bless America" good enough? Not hardly.

I refer you back to the Prophets for proper instructions on how to repent as an individual and as a nation. If G-d's word is true, then repent and obey! If not, then renounce it and burn it! Quit voting G-d and his commandments out of public life, only to cry to that same G-d when the economy gets rocked by the death of a few thousand people in the heart of New York City, or whatever else has happened since then up to this day you are reading this.

I hate the thought of it, but I believe that millions more will die on American soil, if they haven't already by the time you read this, because of our stubbornness and hardness of heart. Our nation will suffer the consequences of our rebellion against G-d.

I do not downplay the tragedy of 9/11. But, think about the cry of all the people around the world, particularly in America. "G-d bless America...." as sung by the U.S. Congress on the steps in a historical moment singing in unison. The nation called together for a "day of prayer and remembrance."

Forgive me for my bluntness, but to borrow a phrase from a Shania Twain song, "that don't impressa me much," says ADONAI Tsva'ot, the Lord of Hosts. As stated before, it is more accurate to call it a "Day of Blaspheme."

Before you get offended by my "in your face" approach to the truth, let me refer you to the "Prophet to the Nations,"

Yirmeyahu (his Hebrew name). Jeremiah says even blunter things than I. No, he's not a bullfrog that sings "Joy to the world." He was called by G-d to be the prophet to the nations of the earth.

As YHVH spoke through Yirmeyahu (Jeremiah), he proclaims to the nations, "Shall I not avenge myself on such a nation as this?"

President George W. Bush said, that under his leadership, America would lead the fight to "rid evil" from the face of the earth. His State of the Union "Axis of Evil" comment received lots of attention. In addition, the President said, "the State of the Union has never been stronger." "Our progress is a tribute...to the might of the U.S. military." "To every enemy of the United States...you will not escape the justice of this nation." "Our cause is just." "Whatever it costs to defend our country, we will pay." "Our enemies believed America was weak and materialistic...they were as wrong as they are evil." After praising Islam and its "tolerance" around the globe, he said, "America will lead by defending liberty and justice, because they are right and true and unchanging for all people everywhere...No nation is exempt."

Your words, Mr. President, speak against you. Your enemies are not wrong, but rather, they are "right as they are evil." "No nation is exempt." How true! America will be held accountable for the evil she has done. We are weak and materialistic and guilty, as they are evil. They too shall be brought to justice, but so shall we!

For you who fear the godless ACLU and their followers, let me refer you to **www.wallbuilders.com** and David Barton, the founder of Wallbuilders. If you don't have a computer, find someone who does and check out their website. Stop being intimidated by those godless lawyers who hate G-d and his commandments. Educate yourselves and tell them you've had enough. David Barton is your man of the hour for understanding our Founding Fathers and their Faith. Learn from him while you are still able.Learn your history the way it happened, not the way it is re-written by those who want to keep you ignorant.

SEE

www. noise of thunder. com
www. adullam films. com

AMERICA'S FOUNDING FATHERS

Contrary to the teaching of President Obama, this nation WAS a YHVH-fearing nation. It WAS a Judeo-Christian nation. Twenty-seven of the fifty-six signers of the Declaration of Independence held Seminary Degrees. What does that tell you about the fable called "separation of church and state"?

Incidentally, the phrase "separation of church and state" is not in the U.S. Constitution. It is in the Constitution of the U.S.S.R (former Soviet Union). I discovered this back in College when I defended Pat Robertson's right to run for President after a foolish school editor stated a minister had no constitutional right to run for office.

During a World View Weekend (see Brannon Howse's **www.worldviewweekend.com** for more information and get your community organized to sponsor one in your area, without haste), David Barton, via video, enlightened me to the following facts, which I now pass on to you.

Mr. Barton quoted a couple of our founding fathers regarding our CHRISTIAN HERITAGE.

According to David Barton (www.wallbuilders.com), John Adams, one of America's founding fathers and second President stated the following:

"The general principles on which society achieves independence are the general principles of Christianity....These general principles of Christianity are as eternal and immutable as the existence and attributes of G-d." - President John Adams

From President James A. Garfield, also an ordained minister:

"Now, more than ever before the people are responsible for the character of their Congress. If that body be ignorant, reckless, and corrupt, it is because the people tolerate ignorance, recklessness, and corruption. If it be intelligent, brave, and pure it is because the people demand these high qualities to represent them in the national legislature. If the next centennial does not

find us a great nation, it will be because those who represent the enterprise, the culture, and the morality of the nation do not aid in controlling the political forces." - President James A. Garfield

I believe President Garfield's words have been evidenced by our recent President Bill Clinton, who has redefined the word "is" for us and shown us that character and morality in our present day do not matter. It is also necessary to remember that it was we the American people who elected him, or allowed him to get elected, twice. Can we claim innocence?

This indifference towards G-d's standards has also been reinforced by many a talk show host, liberal and "conservative," as they proclaim that "character and morality do not matter in the lives of our politicians." What a day we now live in. How can we claim the blessings of the Living G-d when we care not about His standards in the governing of our nation?

"When the righteous flourish, the people rejoice; but when the wicked are in power, the people groan." (Mishlei/Proverbs 29:2)

For those of you who still do not see the connection between our nation's character and greatness and G-d's blessing and protection, let me share another interesting fact, again given me by Mr. David Barton.

On September 6, 1774, at the opening session of the First Congress of the United States, Congress started with a THREE HOUR PRAYER SESSION. This prayer session was not to multiple gods, it was to ONE G-d. This G-d's name was YHVH, whose Son is Yeshua the Messiah. During this prayer session, four chapters of the BIBLE were read and used to guide their prayers.

John Adams felt so strongly that he implored all to read Psalm 35. Since our founding father, John Adams, felt so strongly about it, maybe we should read it here now and see what was so important to this "atheist" (as revisionist historians call the founding fathers and would like to teach our children):

"ADONAI, oppose those who oppose me; fight against those who fight against me. Grasp your shield and protective gear, and rise to my defense. Brandish spear and battle-axe against my pursuers; let me hear you say, 'I am your salvation.'

"May those who seek my life be disgraced and put to confusion; may those who are plotting harm for me be repulsed and put to shame. May they be like chaff before the wind, with the angel of ADONAI to drive them on. May their way be dark and slippery, with the angel of ADONAI to pursue them. For unprovoked, they hid their net over a pit; unprovoked, they dug it for me. May destruction come over him unawares. May the net he concealed catch himself; may he fall into it and be destroyed.

"Then I will be joyful in ADONAI, I will rejoice in his salvation. All my bones will say, 'Who is like you? Who can rescue the weak from those stronger than they, the poor and needy from those who exploit them?'

"Malicious witnesses come forward, asking me things about which I know nothing. They repay me evil for good; it makes me feel desolate as a parent bereaved. But I, when they were ill, wore sackcloth; I put myself out and fasted; I can pray that what I prayed for them might also happen to me. I behaved as I would for my friend or my brother; I bent down in sorrow as if mourning my mother.

"But when I stumble, they gather in glee; they gather against me and strike me unawares; they tear me apart unceasingly. With ungodly mocking and grimacing, they grind their teeth at me. ADONAI, how much longer will you look on? Rescue me from their assaults, save the one life I have from the lions!

"I will give you thanks in the great assembly, I will give you praise among huge crowds of people. Don't let those who are wrongfully my enemies gloat over me; and those who hate me unprovoked -- don't let them smirk at me.

"For they don't speak words of peace but devise ways to deceive the peaceful of the land. They shout to accuse me, 'Aha! Aha! we saw you with our own eyes!' You saw them, ADONAI; don't stay silent. ADONAI, don't stay far away from me.

"Wake up! Get up, my G-d, my Lord! Defend me and my cause! Give judgment for me, ADONAI, my G-d, as your righteousness demands.

"Don't let them gloat over me. Don't let them say to themselves, 'Aha! We got what we wanted!' or say, 'We swallowed them up!' May those who gloat over my distress be *disgraced and humiliated. May those who aggrandize themselves at my expense be covered with shame and confusion.*

"But may those who delight in my righteousness shout for joy and be glad! Let them say always, 'How great is ADONAI, who delights in the peace of his servant!' Then my tongue will tell of your righteousness and praise you all day long." *(Tehillim/Psalms 35)*

Atheist? Hardly.

From Gary DeMar's book, *America's Christian History: The Untold Story* (Atlanta, GA: American Vision Inc., 1995) page 1, comes the following quote:

"I believe no one can read the history of our country without realizing that the Good Book and the spirit of the Savior have from the beginning been our guiding geniuses.... Whether we look to the first charter of Virginia...or to the Charter of New England...or to the Charter of Massachusetts Bay...or to the Fundamental Orders of Connecticut...the same objective is present: A Christian land governed by Christian principles....

"I believe the entire Bill of Rights came into being because of the knowledge our forefathers had of the Bible and their belief in it: freedom of belief, of expression, of assembly, of petition, the dignity of the individual, the sanctity of the home, equal justice under law, and the reservation of powers to the people....

"I like to believe we are living today in the spirit of the Christian religion. I like also to believe that as long as we do so, no great harm can come to our country." - Former Chief Justice Earl Warren, addressing the annual prayer breakfast of the International Council of Christian Leadership, 1954.

I would like to believe no harm can come to our country as well Mr. Chief Justice. But 9/11 has sent a message, loud and clear, that this nation is no longer under G-d's protection. As our current national leadership has proclaimed, this country is no longer a Christian nation. Why then do we marvel that the Creator G-d will not protect us anymore?

"BE" ATTITUDES

Back to the topic of "self-validation." Let me take you on a short journey, if I may.

In order to begin our journey, let us go to Matthew chapter 5 to what are known as the Beatitudes.

Also, let us change the form of the English verb used by Yeshua (who spoke Hebrew) in these verses. "To be" is conjugated as follows: I am; he/she/it is; they are; we are. So let us use "be" as our verb to bring it even closer to home. Thus, I like to call them the "Be" Attitudes. They are more than attitudes. They are more than just an act of thinking, they are states of being (G-d's law on our forehead), demonstrated through our doing (G-d's law on our hand)!

Matthew 5:3-12

"How blessed (BE) the poor in spirit! for the Kingdom of Heaven is theirs." (v.3)

As long as we think that we are "good" and do not need the touch of the Father's hand, then we will not see heaven. Period.

"For you keep saying, 'I am rich, I have gotten rich, I don't need a thing!' You don't know that you are the one who is wretched, pitiable, poor, blind and naked! My advice to you is to buy from me gold refined by fire, so that you may be rich; and white clothing, so that you may be dressed and not have to be ashamed of your nakedness; and eyesalve to rub on your eyes, so that you may see. As for me, I rebuke and discipline everyone I love; so exert yourselves, and turn from your sins! Here, I'm standing at the door, knocking. If someone hears my voice and opens the door, I will come in to him and eat with him, and he will eat with me. I will let him who wins the victory sit with me on my throne, just as I myself also won the victory and sat down with my Father on his throne. Those who have ears, let them hear what the Spirit is saying to the Messianic communities." *(Revelation 3:17-22)*

To be poor in spirit is to acknowledge our inability to pay for, or ransom, ourselves from the prison of sin. We cannot pay our fine. Our sentence is spiritual death.

"For the Torah has in It a shadow of the good things to come, but not the actual manifestation of the originals. Therefore, it can never, by means of the same sacrifices repeated endlessly year after year, bring to the goal those who approach the Holy Place to offer them. Otherwise, wouldn't the offering of those sacrifices have ceased? For if the people performing the service had been cleansed once and for all, they would no longer have sins on their conscience. No, it is quite the contrary -- in these sacrifices is a reminder of sins, year after year. FOR IT IS IMPOSSIBLE THAT THE BLOOD OF BULLS AND GOATS SHOULD TAKE AWAY SINS." (Messianic Jews/Hebrews 10:1-4)

Yet, Yeshua offers to pay our debt for us. By admitting our guilt (sinfulness) and need for someone to pay our fine (a savior), then, and only then are we "poor in spirit" and able to enter into the kingdom of heaven through the Gate, called Yeshua.

"I AM the way -- and the Truth and the Life; no one comes to the Father except through me." (Yochanan/John 14:6)

"Blessed BE the poor in spirit..."

"How blessed (BE) those who mourn! for they will be comforted." (v.4)

As we look to the "snake on a stick," we see that it is the "nails" of our sin that have pegged Him on the tree. We see that our sins have been placed upon the head of the Innocent One. He has taken the punishment that we deserve. He has taken our place on death's deadly stake.

"When that day comes, I will seek to destroy all nations attacking Yerushalayim; and I will pour out on the house of David and on those living in Yerushalayim a spirit of grace and prayer; and they will look to me, whom they pierced. They will mourn for him as one mourns for an only son; they will be in bitterness on his behalf like the bitterness for a firstborn son." (Z'kharyah/Zechariah 12:9, 10)

"But he was wounded because of our crimes, crushed because of our sins; the disciplining that makes us whole fell on him, and by his bruises we are healed." (Yesha'yahu/Isaiah 53:5)

Thus, we are comforted.

"Blessed BE those who mourn..."

"How blessed (BE) the meek! for they will inherit the Land!" (v.5)

In order to see our sin and our need for the Savior, we must be honest with ourselves and with the entire universe.

This can only come about when we look upon the King and see his Holiness. Like the prophet, we then fall in humility on our face and proclaim ourselves unworthy to be in His presence.

"Woe to me! I am doomed! -- because I, a man with unclean lips, living among a people with unclean lips, have seen with my own eyes the King, ADONAI-Tzva'ot!" (Yesha'yahu/Isaiah 6:5)

Unless we become as children who are unconcerned about their "place" in society, and come into the Holy of Holies through the Blood of the Lamb, we cannot receive our inheritance.

"Then I saw a new heaven and a new earth, for the old heaven and the old earth had passed away, and the sea was no longer there. Also I saw the holy city, New Yerushalayim, coming down out of heaven from G-d, prepared like a bride beautifully dressed for her husband. I heard a loud voice from the throne say, 'See! G-d's Sh'khinah is with mankind, and he will live with them. They will be his peoples, and he himself, G-d-with-them, will be their G-d. He will wipe away every tear from their eyes. There will no longer be any death; and there will no longer be any mourning, crying or pain; because the old order has passed away.

"Then the One sitting on the throne said, 'Look! I am making everything new!' Also he said, 'Write, 'These words are true and trustworthy!' And he said to me, 'It is done! I am the 'A' and the 'Z,' the Beginning and the End. To anyone who is thirsty I myself will give water free of charge from the Fountain of Life. He who wins the victory will receive these things, and I will be his G-d, and he will be my son. But as for the cowardly, the untrustworthy, the vile, the murderers, the sexually immoral, those who misuse drugs in connection with the occult, idol-

worshippers, and all liars -- their destiny is the lake burning with fire and sulphur, the second death." (Revelation 21:1-8)

"Blessed BE the meek..."

"How blessed (BE) those who hunger and thirst for righteousness! for they will be filled."(v.6)

Before we can hunger after the things of G-d we must be sick of the things of the world. If our palate still longs after the delicacies of sin, how can we expect to be satisfied with the sweetness of the Savior?

"Taste, and see that ADONAI is good." (Tehillim/Psalms 34:8)

Though, of course, as we have acknowledged our spiritual poverty, and have seen the sinfulness of sin, and have humbled ourselves before the Almighty G-d, we can rest assured that we will now hunger after His righteousness. Thus, we can also rest on His promise that we WILL BE filled.

"Keep asking, and it will be given to you; keep seeking, and you will find; keep knocking, and the door will be opened to you. For every one who keeps asking receives; he who keeps seeking finds; and to him who keeps knocking, the door will be opened. Is there anyone here who, if his son asks him for a loaf of bread, will give him a stone? Or if he asks for a fish, will give him a snake? So if you, even though you are bad, know how to give your children gifts that are good, how much more will your Father in heaven keep giving good things to those who keep asking him!" (Mattityahu/Matthew 7:7-11)

"Blessed BE those who hunger and thirst for righteousness..."

"How blessed (BE) those who show mercy! for they will be shown mercy." (v.7)

How can we claim the forgiveness of G-d, if we are unwilling to forgive others? I believe I have made it clear earlier about the sad witness many professing "Christians" make as they backstab and mock one another through gossip and slander. Will G-d not hold us accountable for our words as well as our deeds?

Our King Yeshua makes this painfully clear in his parable of the unforgiving "forgiven" servant who had just been forgiven of his debts in Matthew 18:21-35.

"This is how my heavenly Father will treat you, unless you each forgive your brother from your hearts." (Mattityahu/Matthew 18:35)

"Human being, you have already been told what is good, what ADONAI demands of you -- no more than to act justly, love grace and walk in purity with your G-d." (Mikhah/Micah 6:8)

"Blessed BE those who show mercy..."

"How blessed (BE) the pure in heart! for they will see G-d." (v.8)

Of course, in ourselves, our hearts are evil and nothing near pure. It is only through the cleansing Blood of the Pesach Lamb, Yeshua, that we are cleansed and made pure.

"For G-d's grace, which brings deliverance, has appeared to all people. It teaches us to renounce godlessness and worldly pleasures, and to live self-controlled, upright and godly lives now, in this age; while continuing to expect the blessed fulfillment of our certain hope, which is the appearing of the Sh'khinah of our great G-d and the appearing of our Deliverer, Yeshua the Messiah. He gave himself up on our behalf in order to free us from all violation of Torah and purify for himself a people who would be his own, eager to do good." (Titus 2:11-14)

Remember, works come AFTER being made pure.

"See what love the Father has lavished on us in letting us be called G-d's children! For that is what we are. The reason the world does not know us is that it has not known him. Dear friends, we are G-d's children now; and it has not yet been made clear what we will become. We do know that when he appears, we will be like him; because we will see him as he really is. And everyone who has this hope in him continues purifying himself, since G-d is pure. Everyone who keeps sinning is violating Torah -- indeed, sin is violation of Torah. You know that he appeared in order to take away sins, and that there is no sin in him. So no one who remains united with him continues sinning; everyone who does continue sinning has neither seen him nor known him.

"Children, don't let anyone deceive you -- it is the person that keeps on doing what is right who is righteous, just as G-d is righteous. The person who keeps on sinning is from the Adversary, because from the very beginning the Adversary has

kept on sinning. It was for this very reason that the son of G-d appeared, to destroy these doings of the Adversary. No one who has G-d as his Father keeps on sinning, because the seed planted by G-d remains in him. That is, he cannot continue sinning, because he has G-d as his Father. Here is how one can distinguish clearly between G-d's children and those of the Adversary: everyone who does not continue doing what is right is not from G-d. Likewise, anyone who fails to keep loving his brother is not from G-d." (1 Yochanan/John 3:1-10)

So do we purify self? No, rather, we accept Messiah's purity and Spirit that enable us to live a pure life. (i.e. "self-validation")

"Blessed BE the pure in heart..."

"How blessed (BE) those who make peace! for they will be called sons of G-d." (v.9)

"Don't suppose that I have come to bring peace to the Land. It is not peace I have come to bring, but a sword!" (Mattityahu/Matthew 10:34)

G-d's peace is not the world's peace. The United Nations speaks of peace, but this is not G-d's peace. Has the UN ever brought peace? Hardly.

"What I am leaving with you is shalom -- I am giving you my shalom. I don't give the way the world gives...." (Yochanan/John 14:27)

The angels proclaimed, *"In the highest heaven, glory to G-d! And on earth, peace among people of good will!" (Luke 2:14)*

This Peace is THE ONLY peace that can wrest free the heart that is unsuccessfully trying to escape the sin that has conquered it and is ruling over it. Allah's "peace" cannot rescue! Buddha's "peace" cannot rescue! The UN's "peace" cannot rescue! No other "peace" can rescue!

YESHUA, THE MESSIAH, IS THE PRINCE OF PEACE who comes in and sets the captives free! The Gospel of Peace is to be proclaimed to all nations.

"How beautiful on the mountains are the feet of him who brings good news, proclaiming shalom, bringing good news of good things, announcing salvation and saying to Tziyon, 'Your G-d is King!'" (Yesha'yahu/Isaiah 52:7)

We are to be peacemakers, by proclaiming to the captives of sin's prison that they can be free!

"Since everyone who calls on the name of ADONAI will be delivered. But how can they call on someone if they haven't trusted in him? And how can they trust in someone if they haven't heard about him? And how can they hear about someone if no one is proclaiming him? And how can people proclaim him unless G-d sends them? -- as the Tanakh puts it, 'How beautiful are the feet of those announcing good news about good things!" (Romans 10:13-15)

As G-d's children, we have a responsibility to share the Gospel with all the hurting hearts around us. It's our purpose, remember!

Even when they clinch their hurts to their chest and refuse our attempts at helping bind up their broken hearts, we are still given the mission to proclaim the Father's message of Love and Peace.

"...All authority in heaven and on earth has been given to me. Therefore, go and make people from all nations into talmidim, immersing them into the reality of the Father, the Son, and the Ruach HaKodesh, and teaching them to obey everything that I have commanded you. And remember! I am with you always, even until the end of the age." (Mattityahu/Matthew 28:18-20)

"Blessed BE those who make peace..."

"How blessed (BE) those who are persecuted because they pursue righteousness! for the Kingdom of Heaven is theirs. How blessed you are when people insult you and persecute you and tell all kinds of vicious lies about you because you follow me!" (v.10, 11)

To rescue a soul from hell is to take a prized possession from the enemy. To dare to believe G-d and keep His commandments is to bring the wrath of the Devil and his armies against us.

Our enemy is not concerned with the slothful soldier (Matthew 24:45-51). Nor, is he angry with the one who is doing more harm than good in G-d's Kingdom (Mark 7:6-9).

Rather, these soldiers are his favorite tools to use in his fight against G-d's "Peace Movement."

But woe to the daring soul that is alert and active for G-d's Kingdom.

"The dragon was infuriated over the woman and went off to fight with the rest of her children, those who obey G-d's commands and bear witness to Yeshua." (Revelation 12:17)

Yeshua tells us that we cannot be neutral. We either serve Him or we serve sin.

"Therefore, there is no longer any condemnation awaiting those who are in union with the Messiah Yeshua. Why? Because the Torah of the Spirit, which produces this life in union with Messiah Yeshua, has set me free from the "Torah" of sin and death. For what the Torah could not do by itself, because it lacked the power to make the old nature cooperate, G-d did by sending his own Son as a human being with a nature like our own sinful one. G-d did this in order to deal with sin, and in so doing he executed the punishment against sin in human nature so that the just requirement of the Torah might be fulfilled in us who do not run our lives according to what our old nature wants but according to what the Spirit wants.

"For those who identify with their old nature set their minds on the things of the old nature, but those who identify with the Spirit set their minds on the things of the Spirit. Having one's mind controlled by the old nature is death, but having one's mind controlled by the Spirit is life and shalom. For the mind controlled by the old nature is hostile to G-d, because it does not submit itself to G-d's Torah -- indeed, it cannot. Thus, those who identify with their old nature cannot please G-d. But you, you do not identify with your old nature but with the Spirit -- provided the Spirit of G-d is living inside you, for anyone who doesn't have the Spirit of the Messiah doesn't belong to him." (Romans 8:1-14)

We are either the Children of G-d or the children of Satan.

"They answered him, 'Our father is Avraham.' Yeshua replied, 'If you are children of Avraham, then do the things Avraham did! As it is, you are out to kill me, a man who has told you the truth which I heard from G-d. Avraham did nothing like that! You are doing the things your father does.' 'We're not illegitimate children!' they said to him. 'We have only one Father

-- G-d!' Yeshua replied to them, 'If G-d were your Father, you would love me; because I came out from G-d; and now I have arrived here. I did not come on my own; he sent me. Why don't you understand what I'm saying? Because you can't bear to listen to my message.

"You belong to your father, Satan, and you want to carry out your father's desires. From the start he was a murderer, and he has never stood by the truth, because there is no truth in him. When he tells a lie, he is speaking in character; because he is a liar -- indeed, the inventor of the lie!

"But as for me, because I tell the truth you don't believe me. Which one of you can show me where I'm wrong? If I'm telling the truth, why don't you believe me? Whoever belongs to G-d listens to what G-d says; the reason you don't listen is that you don't belong to G-d." (John 8:39-47)

To do the will of the Father in Heaven is to make war on Satan. To do the will of the Father is to keep His commandments and to preach the Gospel of Yeshua.

"Next I saw another angel flying in mid-heaven with everlasting Good News to proclaim to those living on the earth -- to every nation, tribe, language and people. In a LOUD voice he said, 'Fear G-d, give him glory, for the hour has come when he will pass judgment! Worship the One who made heaven and earth, the sea and the springs of water!

"Another angel, a second one, followed, saying, 'She has fallen! She has fallen! Bavel the Great! She made all the nations drink the wine of G-d's fury caused by her whoring!

"Another angel, a third one, followed them and said in a loud voice, 'If anyone worships the beast and its image and receives the mark on his forehead or on his hand, he will indeed drink the wine of G-d's fury poured undiluted into the cup of his rage. He will be tormented by fire and sulfur before the holy angels and before the Lamb, and the smoke from their tormenting goes up forever and ever. They have no rest, day or night, those who worship the beast and its image and those who receive the mark of its name.

"This is when perseverance is needed on the part of G-d's people, those who observe his commands and exercise Yeshua's faithfulness..." (Revelation 14:6-12)

"Rejoice, be glad, because your reward in heaven is great -- they persecuted the prophets before you in the same way." (v.12)

So, we see that the beatitudes are life's journey of the child of G-d. They are the daily walk, or daily execution stake, or daily cross, which we are to take up as we follow our Lord and Savior, Yeshua the Messiah. The journey on the path of the Beatitudes is not one of attitude, but of faith.

Look at it like this: If I miss the off-ramp for my destination, I am going the wrong way. Now, I can keep a positive attitude about having missed the turn, but my positive attitude will not get me to my destination.

"There can be a way which seems right to a person, but at its end are the ways of death." (Mishlei/Proverbs 16:25)

On the contrary, Faith is powerful unto salvation. For faith is the substance of things hoped for and the evidence of things unseen. Faith can move mountains.

*"For you have been delivered by grace through trusting, (*not positive attitude)*, and even this is not your accomplishment but G-d's gift. You were not delivered by your own actions: therefore no one should boast. For we are of G-d's making, created in union with the Messiah Yeshua for a life of good actions* (works come after faith, not before)*, already prepared by G-d for us to do." (Ephesians 2:8-10)*

Therefore, let us seek first the Kingdom of G-d and let go of this world's attachments.

"Do not store up for yourselves wealth here on earth, where moths and rust destroy, and burglars break in and steal. Instead, store up for yourselves wealth in heaven, where neither moth nor rust destroys, and burglars do not break in or steal. For where your wealth is, there your heart will be also." (Mattityahu/Matthew 6:19-21)

No, don't quit your job. Don't stop paying your bills and sell your possessions. Don't move to the hilltops and wait for Messiah's return.

But, do let us BE about our Father's business and not our own. Let us make our Father's business our business!

To the Child of G-d and to the sinful soul contemplating coming to the Tree and dying to self, remember the words of our King Yeshua:

"Not everyone who says to me, 'Lord, Lord!' will enter the Kingdom of Heaven, only those who do what my Father in heaven wants. On that Day, many will say to me, 'Lord, Lord! Didn't we prophesy in your name? Didn't we expel demons in your name? Didn't we perform many miracles in your name?' Then I will tell them to their faces, 'I never knew you! Get away from me, you workers of lawlessness!

"So, everyone who hears these words of mine and acts on them will be like a sensible man who built his house on bedrock. The rain fell, the rivers flooded, the winds blew and beat against that house, but it didn't collapse, because its foundation was on rock. But everyone who hears these words of mine and does not act on them will be like a stupid man who built his house on sand. The rain fell, the rivers flooded, the wind blew and beat against that house, and it collapsed -- and its collapse was horrendous!" (Mattityahu/Matthew 7:21-27)

We brought nothing into this world and we will take nothing out.

However, we can take others with us. That is the one "thing" we can take to heaven with us; those people around us, our loved ones, our friends, and the strangers along life's road. What good is it for us to work our lives away for things that matter not?

Think about it. Will the latest hit movie be showing in Heaven? Will there be a Superbowl party with our friends every year? If there is, will our friends be there?

How can they be there if we don't invite them?

Let us not fear what people may say or how they will react. Their hearts are in pain with sin. They have their eyes squeezed closed with pain and their backs to us trying to make it better themselves.

They may scream at us to leave them alone and attack us for daring to put "salt" on the wound. You will be called, "self-righteous" and "holier than thou." It is not you they are yelling at or rejecting. (Matt 10:40, Mark 9:37, Luke 9:48, John 13:20)

But, our King tells us to be salt and light in this dark hurting world.

"You are salt for the Land. But if salt becomes tasteless, how can it be made salty again? It is no longer good for anything except being thrown out for the people to trample on. You are light for the world. A town built on a hill cannot be hidden. Likewise, when people light a lamp, they don't cover it with a bowl, but put it on a lampstand, so that it shines for everyone in the house. In the same way, let your light shine before people, so that they may see the good things you do and praise your Father in heaven." (Mattityahu/Matthew 5:13-16)

There are many who say, "My religion is personal. I don't want to get involved in that hypocritical church stuff."

"Let us continue holding fast to the hope we acknowledge, without wavering; for the ONE who made the promise is trustworthy. And let us keep paying attention to one another, in order to spur each other on to love and good deeds, not neglecting our own congregational meetings, as some have made a practice of doing, but rather, encouraging each other. And let us do this all the more as you see the Day approaching." (Messianic Jews/Hebrews 10:23-25)

The world looks to itself for the answers of life's questions. Science is used by many to explain away G-d. Rejection of truth, G-d's truth, is the way of the world.

The world is N. Y. Twenh. The world is <u>N</u>ot <u>Y</u>eshua, <u>T</u>hat's <u>W</u>hy <u>E</u>veryone <u>N</u>eeds <u>H</u>im!

LOVE HATES

"If someone acknowledges that Yeshua is the Son of G-d, G-d remains united with him, and he with G-d. Also we have come to know and trust the love that G-d has for us. G-d is love; and those who remain in this love remain united with G-d, and G-d remains united with them. Here is how love has been brought to maturity with us: as the Messiah is, so are we in the world. This gives us confidence for the Day of Judgment. There is no fear in love. On the contrary, love that has achieved its goal gets rid of fear, because fear has to do with punishment; the person who keeps fearing has not been brought to maturity in regard to love." (1 Yochanan/John 4:15-18)

In 1 John chapter 4, we are told that G-d is love. Do you agree that G-d is love? I hope so.

There are many other scriptures that speak of G-d's love. In the following scriptures, we are told of things that G-d, who is Love, hates certain things. Let us take a look at what the G-d of Love hates.

"ADONAI tests the righteous; but he hates the wicked and the lover of violence." (Tehillim/Psalms 11:5)

"There six things ADONAI hates, seven which he detests: a haughty look, a lying tongue, hands that shed innocent blood, a heart that plots wicked schemes, feet swift in running to do evil, a false witness who lies with every breath, and him who sows strife among brothers." (Mishlei/Proverbs 6:16-19)

The Scriptures speak much of the things G-d delights in and what he detests. His Torah is full of instructions on what is acceptable and what is not. What is important is that we do not reject G-d's love, nor that we pervert his truth and his commandments.

"Yeshua said, 'I AM the Way -- and the Truth and the Life; no one comes to the Father except through me. Because you have known me, you will also know my Father; from now on, you do

know him -- in fact, you have seen him." *(Yochanan/John 14:6, 7)*

I ask my Jewish and Muslim brothers and sisters of the world, how much clearer can Yeshua (Jesus) get than that? He and the Father are ONE. Thus, we have G-d the Father, G-d the Son, G-d the Holy Spirit. This is the "Trinity." HE IS NOT THREE GODS. HE IS ONE in three persons. It is the only way our finite human minds can grasp the mystery of the Trinity.

"For unto us a child is born, unto us a son is given: and the government shall be upon his shoulder: and his name shall be called Wonderful, Counsellor, The Mighty God, The Everlasting Father, The Prince of Peace. Of the increase of his government and peace there shall be no end, upon the throne of David, and upon his kingdom, to order it, and to establish it with judgment and with justice from henceforth even forever. The zeal of the Lord of Hosts will perform this." *(KJV Isaiah 9:6 & 7)*

And again he says, *"If you love me, you will keep my commands."* *(Yochanan/John 14:15)*

If Jesus were a mere man, he could not claim G-d's commands as his own. Nor could he change them. How much less can a man or group of men change G-d's commands, whether they are in Rome, Mecca, or in Washington D.C.? Yeshua is the I AM.

"Everyone who believes that Yeshua is the Messiah has G-d as his father, and everyone who loves a father loves his offspring too. Here is how we know that we love G-d's children: when we love G-d, we also do what he commands. For loving G-d means obeying his commands. Moreover, his commands are not burdensome, because everything which has G-d as its Father overcomes the world. And this is what victoriously overcomes the world: our trust. Who does overcome the world if not the person who believes that Yeshua is the Son of G-d?

"He is the one who came by means of water and blood, Yeshua the Messiah -- not with water only, but with the water and the blood. And the Spirit bears witness, because the Spirit is the truth. There are three witnesses -- the Spirit, the water and the blood -- and these three are in agreement. If we accept human witness, G-d's witness is stronger, because it is the witness which

G-d has given about his Son. Those who keep trusting in the Son of G-d have this witness in them. Those who do not keep trusting G-d have made him out to be a liar, because they have not trusted in the witness which G-d has given about his Son.

"And this is the witness: G-d has given us eternal life, and this life is in his Son. Those who have the Son have the life; those who do not have the Son of G-d do not have the life. I have written you these things so that you may know that you have eternal life -- you who keep trusting in the person and power of the Son of G-d." (1 Yochanan/John 5:1-13)

"If you keep my commands, you will stay in my love -- just as I have kept my Father's commands and stay in his love." (Yochanan/John 15:10)

Let me set the record straight about something that is of ever increasing importance to the church and society as a whole.

G-d hates evil! Since G-d is love, Love hates evil! G-d hates sin! G-d loves sinners! But, as explained in detail already, sinners must be born again in order to enter heaven.

There is a movement in society that is speaking out against "hate crimes." On the surface this seems very reasonable and righteous. But, take a closer look. It is one thing to stand against racism, but it is totally different to stand against G-d's word.

"Woe to those who call evil good and good evil, who change darkness into light and light into darkness, who change bitter into sweet, and sweet into bitter! Woe to those seeing themselves as wise, esteeming themselves as clever." (Yesha'yahu/Isaiah 5:20-21)

Let me state it again that G-d loves sinners! But He hates sin! If sinners, which we all are without Messiah, repent and ask Messiah to save them of their sin, then G-d will blot out their sins and make them children of G-d. However, IF SINNERS DO NOT REPENT and cry to G-d, then they will die in their sins and will not become children of G-d. Hell is no joke or myth. Hell is real, people of the world. Ignore it and deny it all you want, but G-d isn't kidding about heaven and hell.

When Yeshua refused to cast the stone at the woman caught in adultery, he did not say to her that her sins were forgiven and that it was OK to continue in sin. No. He told her, and all who come to him, "Go, and sin no more."

Why then, do certain people teach that G-d forgives, but does not expect a change in behavior? Nowhere in scripture does G-d teach that it is acceptable to continue in sin! All through the Tenach and New Covenant writings, we are taught to REPENT, T'SHUVA, turn from sin and turn to G-d.

During my college days, I lived with a homosexual. Not in the same room. Three of us shared an apartment, and while living together, his secret was revealed to me. We discussed his struggles and became close friends.

One summer, I worked with some friends from church doing landscaping. One of the guys was a fresh convert into the church out of the gay lifestyle. It wasn't easy for him though.

There was another friend that I remember. He just moved to town and started attending our church. We hit it off and started to hang out. We needed help on the job, so he started working with us. He had already shared with me his first homosexual encounter while attending ORU. Yes, Oral Roberts University. Do you think Christian schools are void of temptation and sin? Wake up!

During my divorce, I had moved back with my mother to try and recoup and make a plan. I got a job delivering pizzas and returned to college to try and make myself more marketable in the workplace.

As I mentioned before, my ex-wife is now an openly practicing homosexual. During this summer, she was still denying her homosexual activity and mindset. Irony of ironies. I thought there was something strange about the manager of this pizza store. She reminded me an awful lot of my ex-wife. Yep. She was living with the female owner who managed another pizza store across town.

There was another girl there who was also a practicing homosexual. And there were two, or more (?), guys who I know were gay.

If I hated homosexuals so much, especially after what my wife was doing to me at the time, do you think I would have worked for and with them?

One of the homosexual guys really liked me. He was always giving me the look. Yeah. The look of desire. No. I did not reciprocate. He told me I was sexy and good-looking. Does that count coming from him?

Even though he made me uncomfortable, I was cordial and continued working there for a few months, until I discovered I could make the same amount of money waiting tables without tearing up my car delivering pizzas.

The point above is to tell my critics that I'm not a homophobe out to destroy homosexuals. I lived with and worked with homosexuals throughout my life.

Regarding sin, when morals go down, defenses do too. Without standards, sensuality leads into more sensuality. Macho men may not want to be called gay, but it does not stop them from experimenting with or practicing homosexuality. Let's stop playing games. Call it what it is my friend. Quit deceiving yourself. Admit your faults and you will find it easier to overcome. The same goes for pornography, another national disgrace.

Maybe you are a practicing homosexual who is reading my book out of curiosity. If so, I'm sure some, if not all of my words have irritated you somewhat.

Before you cry for my downfall and place me on your blacklist, let me ask you a few questions. Why are you so angry? Why do you feel so threatened by me and my words? What is it about the truth in what I say that causes you such pain?

I encourage you to look deep within and ask yourself if you are truly happy and fulfilled without the healing touch of the Redeemer who desires to cleanse you of your sins and heal you of your pains. He knows what was done to you in your past. He knows what you have done in your past. He desires to heal you and make you whole again, unlike those who refuse to help you with your "secrets," but rather insist on dragging you deeper into their dark world.

Stop covering up the darkness. Allow the light of G-d to shine in and the healing touch of the Great Physician perform surgery on your bleeding heart. He knows your pain. Come out of the closet of sin and enter into the world of truth and righteousness, where healing and restoration occur.

Homosexuals are people too. Did you hear me say that one? So that my critics who denounce me for "spreading hate" will know for sure, I said, homosexuals are people too! G-d loves them as much as he loves the heterosexual adulterers and fornicators, upon which, G-d promises that they too will not go unpunished.

"And it is perfectly evident what the old nature does. It expresses itself in sexual immorality, impurity and indecency; idol-worship and misuse of drugs in connection with the occult; in feuding, fighting, becoming jealous and getting angry; in selfish ambition, factionalism, intrigue and envy; in drunkenness, orgies and things like these. I warn you now as I have warned you before: those who do such things will have no share in the Kingdom of G-d!" (Galatians 5:19-21)

Listen. Everyone goes through the identity stage. Particularly in the teen years, we all experience the hormonal changes in our bodies and the questions that come to our minds. Some more than others.

Just because the thoughts come to mind, doesn't make us homosexual. Just because we may be tempted to steal, doesn't make us thieves. Likewise, just because we stole something in the past, doesn't mean we are going to continue to steal in the future.

It's called "Self-control." Self-control is a fruit of the Spirit of G-d. If the Spirit of G-d lives in us and empowers us, then self-control is part of us.

"But the fruit of the Spirit is love, joy, peace, patience, kindness, goodness, faithfulness, humility, self control. Nothing in the Torah stands against such things. Moreover, those who belong to the Messiah Yeshua have put their old nature to death on the stake, along with its passions and desires. Since it is through the Spirit that we have Life, let it also be through the Spirit that we order our lives day by day." (Galatians 5:22-25)

If Yeshua came to set us free from sin, not just the consequences, but the power of sin, then why do people keep excusing it or teaching that it is acceptable to stay in sin? Answer: John 3:19-21.

Are you living with your boyfriend or girlfriend? Get married! Confess your sins to G-d and stop sinning. Are your cheating on your spouse? Stop it! And get right with G-d!

"And this is the message which we have heard from him and proclaim to you: G-d is light, and there is no darkness in him -- none!

"If we claim to have fellowship with him while we are walking in the darkness, we are lying and not living out the truth. But if we are walking in the light, as he is in the light, then we have fellowship with each other, and the blood of his Son Yeshua purifies us from all sin.

"If we claim we have not been sinning, we are making him out to be a liar, and his Word is not in us.

"My children, I am writing you these things so that you won't sin. But if anyone does sin, we have Yeshua the Messiah, the Tzaddik, who pleads our cause with the Father. (NO dead saint or "Virgin" is to be prayed to, ONLY YESHUA). *Also, he is the kapparah for our sins -- and not only for ours, but also for those of the whole world. THE WAY WE CAN BE SURE WE KNOW HIM IS IF WE ARE OBEYING HIS COMMANDS. Anyone who says, 'I know him,' but doesn't obey his commands is a liar the truth is not in him. But if someone does what he says, then truly love for G-d has been brought to its goal in him. This is how we are sure that we are united with him. A person who claims to be continuing in union with him ought to conduct his life the way he did." (1 Yochanan/John 1:5-2:6)*

SELF-CONTROL! We seem to have forgotten that word in society. "It's society's fault or our parents" fault," so we are told.

Nonsense! Our actions are our responsibility. I am responsible for my sin. You are responsible for your sin. We can be influenced, but we decide what action we will take. I know many homosexuals have been abused in their pasts, as well as heterosexuals with "other" immoral problems, but these iniquities do not have to continue on down the line or in your life, especially if you are struggling with something related to your abused background.

1 Corinthians 10:13 tells us that G-d will not allow us to be tempted beyond our ability to withstand it. He gives us the grace,

not to give into it, but to stand against it. GRACE empowers! It not only covers sin, it defends against sin. Titus 2:11-14!

"For G-d's grace, which brings deliverance, has appeared to all people. It teaches us to renounce godlessness and worldly pleasures, and to live self-controlled, upright and godly lives now, in this age; while continuing to expect the blessed fulfillment of our certain hope, which is the appearing of our Deliverer, Yeshua the Messiah. He gave himself up on our behalf in order to free us from all violation of Torah and purify for himself a people who would be his own, eager to do good." (Titus 2:11-14)

Why do I write about this controversial topic? Because, homosexuality and sensuality are on a dangerous rise in society today. We need to stop being "homophobic." When I say homophobic, I mean, fearing homosexual activists. We need to call homosexuality what it is. Perversion! It is not alternative. It is unacceptable. Just as adultery, fornication, and divorce on demand are!

Some argue that G-d made them that way. IF it is so natural, then why do homosexual women have to use the sperm of a male friend to make a baby? Where is the "natural" reproduction in this?

Don't twist G-d's words. Don't call evil good and good evil! Just answer my question, if you can. You can't, because it isn't natural. It's Biology 101. You need an egg and a sperm to reproduce. The egg from a female and sperm from a male. Genesis chapter 1 and 2. You've heard it before, I'll say it again. Adam and Eve, not Adam and Steve.

Homosexuals are acceptable to G-d as are all sinners. But, homosexuality is not acceptable, just as all sin is not.

Adulterers and fornicators, as I was one, are called to G-d to be forgiven and empowered to cease their wicked ways and live righteously. Likewise, homosexuals, gossips, backstabbers, and others are called to be forgiven and empowered to cease their wicked ways.

If you happen to be one who agrees with me about homosexuality being sinful, but think that you need to "bring the wrath of G-d down on their head," I call you to repent of your violent, murderous heart.

James and John wanted to call fire down to destroy the unbelievers. Yeshua said that their desire to destroy them was not of G-d.

"You don't know what Spirit you are of; for the Son of Man did not come to destroy people's lives, but to save." (Luke 9:55, 56)

The Gospel is to be taken to sinners. We are to be messengers of the Gospel, not G-d's wrath. G-d will bring his own wrath when that time comes. In the mean time we are to uphold G-d's law and call men to repentance. We bring the message. The Holy Spirit convicts. G-d will condemn and carry out the sentence himself without our help.

The example of King David is the best example one can find of G-d's grace and love for G-d's law. Read the Psalms.

This one should sound familiar. Let's read it again. If you are convicted of your sins and wish to repent and call upon Yeshua for your salvation, then make this your prayer:

"G-d in your grace, have mercy upon me; in your great compassion, blot out my crimes. Wash me completely from my guilt, and cleanse me from my sin. For I know my crimes, my sin confronts me all the time.

"Against you, you only, have I sinned and what is evil from your perspective; so that you are right in accusing me and justified in passing sentence. True, I was born guilty, was a sinner from the moment my mother conceived me. Still, you want truth in the inner person; so make me know wisdom in my inmost heart.

"Sprinkle me with oregano, and I will be clean; wash me, and I will be whiter than snow. Let me hear the sound of joy and gladness, so that the bones you crushed can rejoice. Turn away your face from my sins, and blot out all my crimes.

"Create in me a clean heart, G-d; renew in me a resolute spirit. Don't thrust me away from your presence, don't take your Ruach Kodesh away from me. Restore my joy in your salvation, and let a willing spirit uphold me.

*"THEN I WILL TEACH THE WICKED YOUR WAYS,
and sinners will return to you. Rescue me from the Guilt of
shedding blood, G-d, G-d of my salvation! Then my tongue will
sing about your righteousness -- ADONAI, open my lips; and my
mouth will praise you.*

*"For you don't want sacrifices, or I would give them; you
don't take pleasure in burnt offerings. My sacrifice to G-d is a
broken spirit, G-d, you won't spurn a broken, chastened heart.*

*"In your good pleasure, make Tziyon prosper; rebuild the
walls of Yerushalayim. Then you will delight in righteous
sacrifices, in burnt offerings and whole burnt offerings; then they
will offer bulls on your altar." (Tehillim/Psalm 51)*

I encourage you to read Psalms 119, thoroughly and slowly.
Chew on it. While you chew and meditate on it, think about the
living Torah, whose name is Yeshua (Salvation). Whenever you
read of G-d's law, think of Yeshua, the living law. Then read the
words of Paul in the letter to the Romans, how he speaks of G-d's
law being "good and holy." How dare you say G-d's law is gone,
done away with, or no longer stands! You contradict the very
teachings of Yeshua himself if you espouse such lies. Yeshua, the
Son, never spoke against, contradicted, replaced, destroyed, or
did away with the instructions of the Father. (I'm talking about
the moral laws, not the ceremonial laws.)

Rather, he upheld, fulfilled, established, reinforced, and
clarified the law of the Father. Did Yeshua really teach anything
"new"? Not at all! Everything he taught came from the Father
and upheld everything the Father spoke to us through Moses.

If you don't believe me, then I challenge you to read the
"Torah" more closely and discover for yourself how much of
what Yeshua taught came from the "law of Moses."

Don't get caught up in the "governmental' aspects of the
laws regarding punishments. Just as we, being citizens of our
country, do not sentence others for their crimes (unless you are a
judge for your career), we are still expected to obey the laws of
the land. Likewise, we do not pronounce sentence and punish the
wicked, but as citizens of G-d's kingdom, we are still expected to
serve him in obedience according to his laws. *"If you love me,
you will keep my commands." (Yochanan/John 14:15)*

To you fellow Gentiles who are grafted in, don't get caught up on the 600+ "Jewish" laws. As grafted in Gentiles, we need to focus on the Ten Words, or Commands, that were written in stone and placed "inside" the ark. Unless you understand and keep these, discussing the rest is a waste of time. When I speak of keeping G-d's law, to you the reader, I am focusing on the Ten Commandments. Do learn, but do not be distracted by the rest. The details of Torah, as applied to Jews and Gentiles, can be studied about as you dig into G-d's Word. Let us not get legalistic over 600 when we don't even uphold the 10.

Note: Paul quotes the Decalogue in Romans 13, which was written to Gentile believers, when he "sums up" the law in loving your neighbor as yourself. It's basic math. To sum up does not mean to take away. Paul, the apostle, did not take away, or replace the law of Yeshua.

"Don't owe anyone anything -- except to love one another; for whoever loves his fellow human being has fulfilled Torah. For the commandments, 'Don't commit adultery,' 'Don't murder,' 'Don't steal,' 'Don't covet,' and any others are summed up in this one rule: 'Love your neighbor as yourself.' Love does not do harm to a neighbor; therefore love is the fullness of Torah." (Romans 13:8-10)

There! Did you catch it! Loving your neighbor is keeping Torah! Can you see it yet?

"Love your neighbor as yourself; I am ADONAI." (Vayikra/Leviticus 19:18)

And neither did Yeshua, the Son, take away or replace the law of the Father.

"Don't think that I have come to abolish the Torah or the Prophets. I have come not to abolish but to complete. Yes indeed! I tell you that until heaven and earth pass away, not so much as a yud or a stroke will pass from the Torah -- not until everything has happened." (Mattityahu/Matthew 5:17, 18)

I don't know about you, but I still walk on earth and look up into the heavens. I guess that means G-d's law still stands. Ya think?

I refer you to a couple of Dr. Brad Young's books, *Paul the Jewish Theologian,* and *Jesus, the Jewish Theologian,*

(Hendrickson Publishers). Dr. Young is President and Founder of the Gospel Research Foundation, which is committed to exploring the Jewish roots of the Christian Faith.

For now, look at it this way. Whenever you hear or read the word Torah, or law in the scriptures, just think of Yeshua being the living Torah. Torah is life. Torah is light. It is good and holy. Yeshua, Salvation, the Living Torah, is life, light, good, and holy.

Just remember, those who escape the mark of the beast in Revelation are not the miracle workers, but the commandment keepers. Chew on that as you rediscover G-d's whole word.

"The dragon was infuriated over the woman and went off to fight the rest of her children, those who obey G-d's commands and bear witness to Yeshua." (Revelation 12:17)

"This is when perseverance is needed on the part of G-d's people, those who observe his commands and exercise Yeshua's faithfulness." (Revelation 14:12)

"They defeated him because of the Lamb's blood and because of the message of their witness. Even when facing death they did not cling to life." (Revelation 12:11)

BE PASSIONATE

I remember watching part of the 2000 Golden Globe Awards and listening to Barbara Streisand talk about someone asking her for advice about whether they should be an actor. She told the audience that if you have to ask, you shouldn't do it. "You should be passionate about it," she said.

How true! Not that Barbara Streisand speaks for G-d, but the words that came out of her mouth were quite accurate.

Do you have to ask G-d what he wants you to do? (Yes, we should consult G-d in our lives, but think about what I am saying here.)

I heard it said of Dave Thomas, founder of the Wendy's hamburger franchise, that he just loved hamburgers. So, he started a restaurant, and the rest is history.

The Colonel, of KFC fame, also started out with an idea that grew beyond his dreams. As with most people, the big comes from the small.

George Muller and D.L Moody had different ideas. They didn't seek after money or fame, but each had a dream that was very simple. They saw a need and did what they could. The rest is history. As well are the stories of Hus, Wycliffe, Fox, Knox, Wesley, Booth, and countless others.

To the scriptures...

The little shepherd boy watched his sheep. When the bear came, he fought and killed it. When the lion came, he fought and killed it. He looked at the stars at night and awed at G-d and His creation. He communed with G-d as a youth watching his sheep.

His focus was on his task at hand and he worshipped G-d, not to make his life better than it was or to change his situation, but he worshipped G-d because, HE IS.

David worshipped G-d for who He was, not for what David hoped to get out of his worship. David made no deals with G-d. He did not worship G-d, say prayers to G-d, do so many Bible studies, attend so many services, or any other "spiritual" activities in an effort to get G-d's attention.

He worshipped the Great I Am because He Is.

David hadn't a clue to G-d's plan. David did not "work" to become G-d's choice as King of Israel. It was probably good that he didn't. Look at what happened to Saul when he took things into his hands and tried to make G-d bless that which G-d did not command. (I Samuel 13)

David was chosen by G-d to be King because of G-d's own reasons. We are told that David was a man after G-d's own heart, but does that mean he was the only one? There may have been others, but G-d chose David because He (G-d) Is.

"Who are you, a mere human being, to talk back to G-d? Will what is formed say to him who formed it, 'Why did you make me this way?' Or has the potter no right to make from a given lump of clay this pot for honorable use and that one for dishonorable?" (Romans 9:20-21)

We will never know and understand the Lord's ways of doing things. Again...We will NEVER know G-d's ways of doing things!

"'For my thoughts are not your thoughts, and my ways are not your ways,' says the Lord. 'As high as the sky is above the earth are my ways higher than your ways, and my thoughts than your thoughts. For just as the rain and snow fall from the sky and do not return there, but water the earth, causing it to bud and produce, giving seed to the sower and bread to the eater; so is my word that goes out from my mouth -- it will not return to me unfulfilled; but it will accomplish what I intend, and cause to succeed what I sent it to do." (Yesha'yahu/Isaiah 55:8-11)

So why do we get so mad at Him when things don't go the way we think they should?

Pride! Arrogance! Selfishness!

The truth of the matter is that when we get angry with G-d, it is because we want it our way. Let's be honest with ourselves. We want G-d to be our personal Burger King. We want to be able to drive up to the window and order it our way and we expect it to be out in 5 minutes or less.

G-d is neither a Santa Clause nor a Burger King!

We cannot expect it the way we pray for it! Nor can we EARN what we pray for!

Don't misunderstand. There are consequences and rewards to be given out for our actions. *"for he will pay back each one according to his deeds." (Romans 2:6)*

But, do not mix up obedience to G-d with praying to G-d and hoping to be good enough to get what you asked for.

*"You did not choose me, I chose you; and I have commissioned you to go and bear fruit, fruit that will last; so that whatever you ask from the Father in my name he may give you." (Yochanan/*John 15:16)

Let me clarify...

If you obey G-d and stay loyal to your spouse, you will reap the benefits that come with fidelity. If you disobey G-d and cheat on your spouse, you will reap the consequences. Look at people you know for examples.

If you murder, you will see the destruction, pain, and consequences of it. Your prayers to G-d to fix your disobedience will not be answered. The law of consequences is in effect no matter how much you pray. You can find forgiveness of your sin, but you will still pay the earthly consequences. So, if you are on death row for murder, then accept your earthly consequences. If you have truly given your life to the Messiah, then you should not fear your appointed "exodus" from this earth.

If you make a bad investment that you knew was bad, you can find forgiveness, but you've lost your money and have to live with that loss. Radio talk show host, Dave Ramsey calls this a "stupid tax." I'm still paying for my "stupid taxes." May G-d bless me and you with Dave Ramsey's wisdom and self-control regarding our finances.

Being good does not increase your "good" standing with G-d. You cannot earn G-d's forgiveness. You can earn his respect and trust, but not his forgiveness. Don't believe me? How many disciples did Yeshua have? Which ones where closer to him?

Question: Were they "more forgiven or righteous" than the others?

Answer: No. They were all in equal standing regarding their righteousness.

"All have sinned and come short of earning G-d's praise."
(Romans 3:23)

And all who call upon Yeshua are made righteous.

"But G-d demonstrates his own love for us in that the Messiah died on our behalf while we were still sinners."
(Romans 5:8)

"Therefore, if anyone is united with the Messiah, he is a new creation -- the old has passed; look, what has come is fresh and new!" (2 Corinthians 5:17)

So, what made them so special?

Let's refer to a conversation between Yeshua and Peter about this very question... (John 21:20-23) Peter was asking about another disciple. Yeshua responded with "that's none of your business."

Of course that is a paraphrase, but look at it. That's pretty much the gist of it. "What is that to you?" Just another way of saying, "it's none of your business what I decide to do with him. You follow me and don't worry about him."

G-d is G-d. Who are we to question His decisions and plans? Look at it from another perspective.

When I was in the military, I hated not knowing what our commanders were doing. In my mind, not verbally, I questioned their leadership and wondered if they knew what they were doing.

But, what place was it of mine to tell the commanders how to do their job. Besides, they had a better view of things than I. I was just an enlisted soldier in one location on the battle lines. I only saw one small part of the battle. They saw many more parts and had a much better view of the battle at large.

So when they ordered me to move, should I have obeyed or demanded an explanation first? If I had waited for an explanation, I probably would have been killed. If I had survived, I would surely have been court-martialed. And, I would not have "contributed" to the victory. (Luckily, it was only a training exercise.)

Would having an explanation of my orders helped me accomplish my mission? No. I had what I needed to accomplish my mission. I had my orders. My orders were to do MY part. As

I did my part and the other soldiers did their part, the mission's parts came together and resulted in victory.

Likewise, do we have to be in G-d's command center and see what He sees before we can "carry out our orders"?

"Human being, you have already been told what is good, what ADONAI demands of you -- no more than to act justly, love grace and walk in purity with your G-d." (Mikhah/Micah 6:8)

What is the purpose of life? You just read it. Do justly, love mercy, and walk humbly with G-d! Receive G-d's grace through Yeshua and share Him with your neighbor.

Why then do we complicate things? Look into yourself and don't be afraid to go after the desires of your heart.

Have angels visited you? Has G-d burned a bush and spoken audibly to you? Has G-d taken you to heaven and given you a tour?

Why then, do you wait for it to happen? We have our orders in Matthew 28:18-20. They are called the Great Commission. Go!

"A person may plan his path, but ADONAI directs his steps." (Mishlei/Proverbs 16:9)

Look at the many examples in the Bible about how people planned for one direction, but G-d directed them to another.

One example: Paul and his companions were headed towards Asia, but the Lord directed them to Macedonia. (Acts 16:6-10) Did Paul know that he would accomplish as much as he did and be the most quoted New Covenant writer? I don't think so. Did he need to know the results of his efforts? No. He followed the leading of G-d and spread the Gospel wherever he was, including jail. No place was too small; no person was too important or unimportant. All were in need of the Good News.

Back to the Old Covenant writings... Remember the Tabernacle? Who made it? Were they less important than Moses? If it weren't for them, Moses and G-d wouldn't have had a meeting place. Were the builders of the tabernacle less important or less righteous than Moses and the others that ministered within the tabernacle?

G-d had chosen them by name to make the tabernacle. (Exodus 31:1-6) G-d gave them knowledge and understanding of those skills they needed to accomplish the task assigned to them. Let us beware, lest we think "we" are responsible for our knowledge and understanding of the world around us.

As much as I disagree with President Bush's and President Obama's love for Islam and Allah, I still believe G-d had more to do with their elections than either would like to admit publicly. That doesn't mean they were/are perfect, or even under G-d's blessings. Even Paul told us to follow him as he follows the Messiah. So, do the President and others follow Messiah? Ok. I'm with him. Follows Allah? Sorry, no can do. That's forbidden by YHVH, the G-d of Abraham, Isaac, and Jacob.

We know what we know and have what we have only because Creator G-d has allowed us to. Governor Ventura, do you still think G-d has nothing to do with your life's accomplishments? I encourage you and others out there to read the conversation Pilate had with Yeshua. (John 18:28-19:11)

Verse 11 is one to remember, you people who think you are where you are because of your own efforts: *"You would have no power over me if it hadn't been given to you from above;"*

Did Moshe seek to be the Moses we know? To the contrary, he tried to shirk the position off to someone else. He actually angered the Lord by trying to remind G-d of his inadequacies. (Exodus 4:13-14)

Before we look down the nose at the arrogant soul who thinks he is strong enough to exist without G-d, let us not be so self-centered that we continue to see ourselves as inadequate. Rather, let us see Messiah who lives in us, adequate, validated, and victorious.

"Therefore, if anyone IS united with Messiah, he is a new creation -- the old has passed; look, what has come is fresh and new!

"And it is all from G-d, who through the Messiah has reconciled us to himself and has given us the work of that reconciliation:

"which is what G-d in the Messiah was reconciling mankind to himself, not counting their sins against them, and entrusting to us the message of reconciliation.

"Therefore we are ambassadors of the Messiah; in effect, G-d is making his appeal through us. What we do is appeal on behalf of the Messiah, 'Be reconciled to G-d!

"G-d made this sinless man be a sin offering on our behalf, so that in union with him we might fully share in G-d's righteousness." (2 Corinthians 5:17-21)

Chart a course and go! Yes, pray first. But, when you have prayed and sought counsel from those you trust, go! Go and be passionate and unapologetic. Walk according to G-d's word. Many will critique, but none will do it for you. If I had listened to my critics, you wouldn't be reading this book.

STAND!

"Finally, grow powerful in union with the Lord, in union with his mighty strength! Use all the armour and weaponry that G-d provides, so that you will be able to stand against the deceptive tactics of the Adversary.

"FOR WE ARE NOT STRUGGLING AGAINST HUMAN BEINGS, but against rulers, authorities and cosmic powers governing this darkness, against the spiritual forces of evil in the heavenly realm.

"So take up every piece of war equipment G-d provides; so that when the evil day comes, you will be able to resist; and when the battle is won, you will still be standing..

"Therefore, stand! Have the belt of truth buckled around your waist, put on righteousness for a breastplate, and wear on your feet the readiness that comes from the Good News of shalom.

"Always carry the shield of trust, with which you will be able to extinguish all the flaming arrows of the Evil One. And take the helmet of deliverance; along with the sword given by the Spirit, that is, the Word of G-d;

"As you pray at all times, with all kinds of prayers and requests, in the Spirit, vigilantly and persistently, for all G-d's people." (Ephesians 6:10-18)

When it is all said and done, after the book is closed and placed on the shelf, what is there to do, but stand!

If you haven't met Yeshua before reading this book, I hope you have by now.

For all my fellow Eagles, I hope you have been encouraged in your walk of faith. The journey seems long, but it really isn't when you put it into proper perspective.

The closer we look at ourselves, the longer it seems. I encourage you to look to Messiah and you will discover it is shorter and easier than you think.

Look around you. See all the pain around you. You are not alone. By helping others, we get our focus off ourselves. By helping others, we are helping Yeshua.

Do what you can. Every little bit adds up. Most often a smile does more to light someone's world than does giving them a million dollars. If money and things were the cure to life's pain, don't you think Jesus would have preached it so?

I've met many who struggle with things that have been shared in this book. As a matter of fact, I haven't met anyone who hasn't experienced suffering or doubt in their lives. This is not an American issue. It is a universal human issue. YHVH's Kingdom is universal and His order of things is the True World Order of Peace.

I look to the people of the Bible as sources of inspiration. I encourage you to do the same. For example: Joseph is my favorite. When reading his story, I see a happy-go-lucky kind of guy. He seemed to be someone of great innocence. I saw in him a love for life and family that did not suspect what was to come upon him.

He loved and trusted his brothers. He had a great sense of family and worshipped his maker.

However, his faith in his family was shattered one day. Out of jealousy, His brothers tried to kill him. Luckily one of his brothers felt guilty enough to prevent the murder. Instead, they sold him off to slavery in Egypt.

The story in the Bible reads really fast. It speeds through his life from one event to the other. But, stop and think about what he must have been thinking during each of those moments in time and the moments in between.

Can you imagine what he was feeling as he was being dragged behind the camel with the dust flying in his face and the hot sun beating on his head after his own flesh and blood having betrayed him?

What about the time after being thrown into prison for something he didn't do? He was faithful to G-d, but now found his freedom restricted even more and his reputation destroyed.

What about the years he spent contemplating life after the butler promised to remember him, only to forget him? Yet, we are told he did what he was able and was respected for it. He kept his faith in G-d, and after many years of suffering, he was lifted up in honor.

We may not be lifted to power as Joseph was, but we can be assured that we will find rest from our labors when Yeshua comes to take us home.

My wife and I are constantly encouraging one another. Every day is a new day. The struggle, however, is constant. Some days are valley days, while others are mountain top days. Most are spent climbing the mountain. Some days, I encourage her. Some days, she encourages me.

I've often told her what I tell you now. Among other things that I tell myself to keep me in the battle, is that if I wind up in hell, it won't be without a fight.

Not what you expected, is it?

When the devil gets the best of me, when I feel my lowest and wonder if it's worth it, I tell myself and the enemy that I'm not giving up.

"If you're right, Devil, and G-d doesn't want me, then He will have to tell me himself after I've lived out my life. In the mean time, I am going to do my best with what I have and walk by faith believing that G-d does want me. I choose to believe the words of Yeshua instead of you. I will walk in faith that Yeshua's blood is good enough to save me. I claim the blood of Yeshua as my inheritance to eternal life. I am valid, not because of myself, but because of Messiah who lives in me and through me."

"So then, since we are surrounded by such a great cloud of witnesses, let us, too, put aside every impediment -- that is, the sin which easily hampers our forward movement -- and keep running with endurance in the contest set before us, looking away to the Initiator and Completer of that trusting, Yeshua -- who, in exchange for obtaining the joy set before him, endured execution on a stake as a criminal, scorning the shame, and has sat down at the right hand of the throne of G-d.

"Yes, think about him who endured such hostility against himself from sinners, so that you won't grow tired or become despondent. You have not yet resisted to the point of shedding blood in the contest against sin.

"Also you have forgotten the counsel which speaks with you as sons: 'My son, don't despise the discipline of ADONAI or become despondent when he corrects you. For ADONAI disciplines those he loves and whips everyone he accepts as a son.'

"Regard your endurance as discipline; G-d is dealing with you as sons. For what son goes undisciplined by his father? All legitimate sons undergo discipline; so if you don't, you're a mamzer and not a son!

"Furthermore, we had physical fathers who disciplined us, and we respected them; how much more should we submit to our spiritual Father and live! For they disciplined us only for a short time and only as best they could; but he disciplines us in a way that provides genuine benefit to us and enables us to share in his holiness.

"Now, all discipline, while it is happening, does indeed seem painful, not enjoyable; but for those who have been trained by it, it later produces its peaceful fruit, which is righteousness. So, strengthen your drooping arms, and steady your tottering knees; and make a level path for your feet; so that what has been injured will not get wrenched out of joint but rather will be healed.

"Keep pursuing shalom with everyone and the holiness without which no one will see the Lord. See to it that no one misses out on G-d's grace, that no root of bitterness springing up causes trouble and thus contaminates many, and that no one is sexually immoral, or godless like Esav, who in exchange for a single meal gave up his rights as the firstborn. For you know that afterwards, when he wanted to obtain his father's blessing, he was rejected; indeed, even though he sought it with tears, his change of heart was to no avail.

"For you have not come to a tangible mountain, to an ignited fire, to darkness, to murk, to a whirlwind, to the sound of a shofar, and to a voice whose words made the hearers beg that no further message be given to them for they couldn't bear what was being commanded them, 'If even a beast touches the mountain, it is to be stoned to death'; and so terrifying was the sight that Moshe said, 'I am quaking with dread.'

"On the contrary, you have come to Mount Tziyon, that is, the city of the living G-d, heavenly Yerushalayim; to myriads of angels in festive assembly; to a community of the firstborn whose names have been recorded in heaven; to a Judge who is G-d of everyone; to spirits of righteous people who have been brought to the goal; to the mediator of a new covenant, Yeshua; and to the sprinkled blood that speaks better things than that of Hevel.

"See that you don't reject the One speaking! For if those did not escape who rejected him when he gave divine warning on earth, think how much less we will escape if we turn away from him when he warns from heaven. Even then, his voice shook the earth; but now, he has made this promise:

"One more time I will shake not only the earth, but heaven too!"

" And this phrase, 'one more time,' makes clear that the things shaken are removed, since they are created things, so that the things not shaken may remain. Therefore, since we have received an unshakable Kingdom, let us have grace, through which we may offer service that will please G-d, with reverence and fear. For indeed,

"Our G-d is a consuming fire!" (Messianic Jews/Hebrews 12)

One of my favorite songs states the walk of faith in another way.

"There is a supernatural Power
In this mighty river's flow
It can bring the dead to life
And it can fill an empty soul
And give a heart the only thing
Worth living and worth dying for, yeah
But we will never know the awesome power
Of the grace of G-d
Until we let ourselves get swept away
Into this holy flood
So if you'll take my hand
We'll close our eyes and count to three
And take the leap of faith
Come on let's go...

The river's deep, the river's wide, the river's water is alive
So sink or swim, I'm diving in..."
- Steven Curtis Chapman, from his song "Dive"

Therefore, when all is said and done, Stand! And Dive!

Pass this book on to another "Turkey," or an "Eagle" you think might be having difficulty in flying these days.

One more scripture before we read the words of the Prophets to the nations. As the days grow darker before us as this Age comes to a close, and the Dawn of G-d's New Age approaches, let us not forget the words of our Redeemer and Messiah as he spoke them through Yochanan. Do not give up! Overcome to the end!

"These words are true and trustworthy: ADONAI, G-d of the spirits of the prophets, sent his angel to show his servants the things that must happen soon. Look! I am coming very soon Blessed is the person who obeys the words of the prophecy written in this book! (G-d's Word)

"Then I, Yochanan, the one hearing and seeing these things, when I heard and saw them, I fell down to worship at the feet of the angel showing them to me. But he said to me, 'Don't do that! I am only a fellow-servant with you and your brothers, the prophets and the people who obey the words in this book. Worship G-d!'

"Then he said to me, 'Don't seal up the words of the prophecy in this book, because the time of their fulfillment is near. Whoever keeps acting wickedly, let him go on acting wickedly whoever is filthy, let him go on being made filthy. Also, whoever is righteous, let him go on doing what is righteous, and whoever is holy, let him go on being made holy.'

"'Pay attention!' says Yeshua, 'I am coming soon, and my rewards are with me to give to each person according to what he has done. I am the 'A' and the 'Z,' the First and the Last, the Beginning and the End.'

"How blessed are those who wash their robes, so that they have the right to eat from the Tree of Life and go through the gates into the city! Outside are the homosexuals, those who misuse drugs in connection with the occult, the sexually immoral, murderers, idol-worshippers, and everyone who loves and

practices falsehood. I, Yeshua, have sent my angel to give you this testimony for the Messianic communities. I am the Root and Offspring of David, the bright Morning Star. The Spirit and the Bride say, 'Come!' Let anyone who hears say, 'Come!' And let anyone who is thirsty come let anyone who wishes, take the water of life free of charge.

"I warn everyone hearing the words of the prophecy in this book that if anyone adds to them, G-d will add to him the plagues written in this book. And if anyone takes anything away from the words in the book of this prophecy, G-d will take away his share in the Tree of Life and the holy city, as described in this book. The one who is testifying to these things says, 'Yes, I am coming soon!'

"Amen! Come, Lord Yeshua! May the grace of the Lord Yeshua be with all!" (Revelation 22:6-21)

TO THE LAW AND THE TESTIMONY

Who am I that you should listen to me? Let us consult the prophets of old to see if this book you have just read is in line with G-d's word. Judge the words of anyone, including the President, the Pope, or any other political or religious leader. If they do not line up with G-d's word, then do not listen to them, no matter how nice they are or how charismatic they are.

Believer, pray for G-d's perspective before you continue. After you finish this book, I encourage you to read the previous chapters again and grab onto G-d with all your heart and might.

Some say to use honey to attract the bees. I say to you, America, Billy Graham gave you honey, and still you would not come. Soon the "Honey Graham" will sleep with his fathers and the honeycomb will become bitter in your belly. Now, I give you smoke with hopes to smoke you out of the blazing building. If you will not hearken to the warnings of G-d, then you will perish in the flames. Blow the Shofar! Sound the alarm! Call the assembly and the nation to repentance!

You claim the blessings of Israel? How then can you avoid the judgments as well when you rebel against the G-d of Israel? As President Bush proclaimed, "No nation is exempt."

G-d said to Jeremiah, *"I have appointed you to be a prophet to the nations."* Therefore, let us recall the words of this prophet to the nations and see if they speak to us today:

"I will summon all the families in the kingdoms of the north,' says ADONAI, 'and they will come and sit, each one, on his throne at the entrance to the gates of Yerushalayim, opposite its walls, all the way around, and opposite all the cities of Y'hudah. I will pronounce my judgments against them for all their wickedness in abandoning me, offering incense to other gods and worshipping what their own hands made." (Yirmeyahu 1:15-16)

"Haven't you brought this on yourself by abandoning ADONAI your G-d when he led you along the way? If you go to

Egypt, what's in it for you?...Your own wickedness will correct you, your own backslidings will convict you; you will know and see how bad and bitter it was to abandon ADONAI your G-d, and how fear of me is not in you,' says ADONAI Elohim-Tzva'ot." (2:17-19)

"For they have turned their backs to me instead of their faces. But when trouble comes, they will plead, 'Rouse yourself and save us!' Where are your gods that you made for yourselves? Let them save you when trouble comes." (2:27-28)

"Raise your eyes to the bare hills, take a look: where have you not had sex? You sat by the roadsides waiting for them like a nomad in the desert. You have defiled the land with your prostitution and wickedness." (3:2)

"Return, backsliding children and I will heal your backsliding." (3:22)

"Your own ways and your actions have brought these things on yourselves. This is your wickedness, so bitter! It has reached your very heart." (4:18)

"It is because my people are foolish -- they do not know me; they are stupid children, without understanding, wise when doing evil; but they don't know how to do good." (4:22)

"The whole land will be desolate (although I will not destroy it completely). Because of this, the land will mourn and the sky above be black; for I have spoken, I have decided, I will not change my mind, I will not turn back." (4:27, 28)

"Why should I forgive you? Your people have abandoned me and sworn by non-gods. When I fed them to the full, they committed adultery, thronging to the brothels. They have become like well-fed horses, lusty stallions, each one neighing after his neighbor's wife. Should I not punish for this? asks ADONAI. Should I not be avenged on a nation like this?" (5:7-9)

"They have denied ADONAI, they have said, 'He won't do anything, calamity will not strike us, we will see neither sword nor famine. The prophets are merely wind, they do not have the word; the things that they are predicting will happen only to them." (5:12, 13)

"Hear this, stupid, brainless people, who have eyes but do not see, who have ears but do not hear: Don't you fear me? --

says ADONAI. Won't you tremble at my presence? I made the shore the limit for the sea; by eternal decree it cannot pass. Its waves may toss, but to no avail; although they roar, they cannot cross it. But this people has a rebellious, defiant heart; they have rebelled and gone! They don't say to themselves, 'Let's fear ADONAI our G-d, who gives the fall and spring rains in season, who reserves us the weeks assigned for harvest.' Your crimes have overturned nature's rules, your sins have kept back good from you." (5:21-25)

"Should I not punish for this? asks ADONAI. Should I not be avenged on a nation like this? A shocking and horrifying thing has happened in the land: The prophets prophesy lies, the cohanim obey the prophets, and my people love it that way. But what will you do at the end of it all?" (5:29-31)

"They should be ashamed of their detestable deeds, but they are not ashamed at all; they don't know how to blush. Therefore when others fall, they too will fall; when I punish them, they will stumble,' says ADONAI." (6:15)

"Look! You are relying on deceitful words that can't do you any good. First you steal, murder, commit adultery, swear falsely, offer to Ba'al and go after other gods that you haven't known. Then you come and stand before me in this house that bears my name and say, 'we are saved' – so that you can go on doing these abominations!" (7:8-10)

"Therefore, here is what ADONAI Elohim says: 'My anger and fury will be poured out on this place, on men, animals, trees in the fields and produce growing from the ground; and it will burn without being quenched." (7:20)

"This is the nation that has not listened to the voice of ADONAI their G-d. They won't take correction; faithfulness has perished; it has vanished from their mouths." (7:28)

"Prophets and cohanim alike all practice fraud – they dress the wound of the daughter of my people, but only superficially, saying, 'There is perfect shalom,' when there is no shalom. They should be ashamed of their detestable deeds, but they are not ashamed at all, they don't know how to blush. So when others fall, they too will fall; when I punish them, they will stumble." (8:10-12)

"Who is wise enough to understand this? To whom has the mouth of ADONAI spoken, so that he can proclaim it? Why has the land perished and been laid waste like a desert, so that no one passes through?' ADONAI answers: **'Because they abandoned my Torah, which I set before them, and neither listened to what I said nor lived accordingly, but have lived by their own hearts' stubbornness and by the ba'alim, as their ancestors taught them** -- therefore,' says ADONAI-Tzva'ot, the G-d of Isra'el: 'I will feed this people bitter wormwood and give them poisonous water to drink."* (9:12-15)

"The wise man should not boast of his wisdom, the powerful should not boast of his power, the wealthy should not boast of his wealth; instead, let the boaster boast about this: that he understands and knows me -- that I am ADONAI, practicing grace, justice and righteousness in the land; for in these things I take pleasure,' says ADONAI." (9:23, 24)

"Ya'akov's portion is not like these, for he is the one who formed all things, Isra'el is the tribe he claims as his heritage; ADONAI-Tzva'ot is his name." (10:16)

"Pour out your anger on the nations that do not acknowledge you, also on the families that do not call on your name. For they have consumed Ya'akov -- consumed him and finished him off, and laid waste to his home." (10:25)

"...conspiracy. They have returned to the sins of their ancestors, who refused to hear my words, and they have gone after other gods to serve them....I am going to bring on them a disaster which they will not be able to escape; and even if they cry to me, I will not listen to them." *(11:9-11)*

"Here is what ADONAI says: 'As for all my evil neighbors who encroach on the heritage I gave to my people Isra'el as their possession, I will uproot them from their own land, and I will uproot Y'hudah from among them. Then, after I have uprooted them, I will take pity on them again and bring them back, each one to his inheritance, each one to his own land. Then, if they will carefully learn my people's ways, swearing by my name, 'As ADONAI lives,' just as they taught my people to swear by Ba'al, they will be built up among my people. But if

they refuse to listen, then I will uproot that nation, uproot and destroy it,' says ADONAI." (12:14-17)

"Don't pray for this people or for their welfare. When they fast, I will not hear their cry... Rather, I will destroy them with war, famine and disease. Then I said, **'ADONAI, G-d! The prophets are telling them, 'You won't see war, and you won't have famine; but I will give you secure peace in this place.' ADONAI replied, 'The prophets are prophesying lies in my name. I didn't send them, order them or speak to them. They are prophesying false visions to you, worthless divinations, the delusions of their own minds. Therefore,' ADONAI says, 'concerning the prophets who prophesy in my name, whom I did not send... it will be war and famine that will destroy those prophets."** (14:11-15)

"Those destined for death -- to death!
"Those destined for the sword -- to the sword!
"Those destined for famine -- to famine!
"Those destined for captivity -- to captivity!" (15:2)

"A curse on the person who trusts in humans, who relies on merely human strength, whose heart turns away from ADONAI...Blessed is the man who trusts in ADONAI; ADONAI will be his security." (17:5, 7)

"At one time, I may speak about uprooting, breaking down and destroying a nation or kingdom; but if that nation turns from their evil, which prompted me to speak against it, then I relent concerning the disaster I had planned to inflict on it. Similarly, at another time, I may speak about building and planting a nation or kingdom; but if it behaves wickedly from my perspective and doesn't listen to what I say, then I change my mind and don't do the good I said I would do that would have helped it." (18:7-10)

"Sing to ADONAI! Praise ADONAI! For he rescues those in need from the clutches of evildoers." (20:13)

"Take this cup of the wine of fury from my hand, and make all the nations where I am sending you drink it. They will drink, stagger to and fro and behave like crazy people because of the sword that I will send among them...indeed, all the kingdoms of the world that there are on the surface of the earth. **And the king of Sheshakh will drink last of all...if I am bringing disaster on** *the city that bears my own name, do you expect to go unpunished? Yes, I will summon a sword for all the inhabitants of the earth,' says ADONAI."* (25:15-29)

"For the day is coming,' says ADONAI, ' when I will reverse the exile of my people Isra'el and Y'hudah,' says ADONAI, 'I will cause them to return to the land I gave their ancestors, and they will take possession of it.' These are the words ADONAI spoke concerning Isra'el and Y'hudah: Here is what ADONAI says:

"We have heard a cry of terror, of fear and not of peace. Ask now and see: can men give birth to children? Why, then, do I see all the men with their hands on their stomachs like women in labor, with every face turned pale? **How dreadful that day will be! -- there has never been one like it: a time of trouble for Ya'akov, but out of it he will be saved.**

"On that day,' says ADONAI-Tzva'ot, 'I will break his yoke from off your neck, I will snap your chains. Foreigners will no longer enslave him. Instead, they will serve ADONAI their G-d and David their king, whom I will raise up for them.

"So don't be afraid, Ya'akov my servant,' says ADONAI, 'or be alarmed, Isra'el; for I will return you from far away and your offspring from their country of exile. Ya'akov will again be quiet, at rest; and no one will make him afraid.

"For I am with you to save you,' says ADONAI, 'I will finish off all the nations where I have scattered you. However, you I will not finish off, but will discipline only as you deserve; I will not completely destroy you."

"For here is what ADONAI says; 'Your wound is past healing, your injury most severe; no one thinks your wound can be bandaged; you have no medicines that can heal you. All your friends have forgotten you, they no longer seek you out. I have struck you down as an enemy would, punished as a cruel man would, because of your great wickedness, because of your many sins. Why cry that your wound and pain are past healing? I have done these things to you because of your great wickedness, because of your many sins.

"But all who devour you will be destroyed, all your enemies will go into exile, those who plunder you will be plundered,

those who pillage you will be pillaged. For I will restore your health, I will heal you of your wounds,' says ADONAI, 'because they called you an outcast, Tziyon, with no one who cares about her." (30:3-17)

"In the acharit-hayamim, you will understand." (30:24)

*"Here, the days are coming,' says ADONAI, 'when I will make a **new covenant** with the house of Isra'el and with the house of Y'hudah. It will not be like the covenant I made with their fathers on the day I took them by their hand and brought them out of the land of Egypt; because they, for their part, violated my covenant, even though I, for my part, was a husband to them,' says ADONAI.*

"For this is the covenant I will make with the house of Isra'el after those days,' says ADONAI: 'I will put my Torah within them and write it on their hearts; I will be their G-d, and they will be my people." (31:31-33)

"If these laws leave my presence,' says ADONAI, 'then the offspring of Isra'el will stop being a nation in my presence forever.' This is what ADONAI says, 'If the sky above can be measured and the foundations of the earth be fathomed, then I will reject all the offspring of Isra'el for all that they have done,' says ADONAI." (31:36, 37)

"Haven't you noticed that these people are saying, 'ADONAI has rejected the two families he chose'? Hence they despise my people and no longer look at them as a nation. Here is what ADONAI says: 'If I have not established my covenant with day and night and fixed the laws for sky and earth, then I will also reject the descendants of Ya'akov and of my servant David, not choosing from his descendants people to rule over the descendants of Avraham, Yis'chak and Ya'akov. For I will cause their captives to come back, and I will show them compassion." (33:24-26)

Now let us hear a few words from Yesha'yahu, aka Isaiah:

*"For a child is born to us, **a son is given to us**; dominion will rest on his shoulders, and **he will be given the name** Pele-Yo'etz El Gibbor Avi-'Ad Sar-Shalom [Wonder of a counselor, **Mighty G-d**, Father of Eternity, Prince of Peace], in order to extend the dominion and perpetuate the peace of the throne and*

kingdom of David, to secure it and sustain it through justice and righteousness henceforth and forever. The zeal of ADONAI-Tzva'ot will accomplish this." (Yesha'yahu 9:6, 7)

"See, G-d is my salvation. I am confident and unafraid; for Yah ADONAI is my strength and my song, and he has become my salvation!" (11:2)

"Listen! The uproar of the kingdoms of the nations gathering together! ADONAI-Tzva'ot is mustering an army for war...I will punish the world for its evil and the wicked for their iniquity. I will end the arrogance of the proud and humble the insolence of tyrants." (13:4, 11)

"For ADONAI will have compassion on Ya'akov -- he will once again choose Isra'el and resettle them in their own land, where foreigners will join them, attaching themselves to the house of Ya'akov." (14:1)

"Dammesek will soon stop being a city; it will become a heap of ruins." (17:1)

"If you make yourselves stupid, you will stay stupid! If you blind yourselves, you will stay blind! You are drunk, but not from wine; you are staggering, but not from strong liquor. For ADONAI has poured over you a spirit of lethargy; he has closed your eyes (that is, the prophets) and covered your heads (that is, the seers).

"For you this whole prophetic vision has become like the message in a sealed up scroll. When one gives it to someone who can read and says, 'Please read this,' he answers, 'I can't, because it's sealed.' If the scroll is given to someone who can't read with the request, 'Please read this,' he says, 'I can't read.'

"Then ADONAI said: **'Because these people approach me with empty words, and the honor they bestow on me is mere lip-service; while in fact they have distanced their hearts from me, and their 'fear of me' is just a mitzvah of human origin -- therefore, I will have to keep shocking these people with astounding and amazing things, until the 'wisdom' of their 'wise ones' vanishes, and the 'discernment' of their 'discerning ones' is hidden away.'**

"Woe to those who burrow down deep to hide their plans from ADONAI! They work in the dark and say to themselves,

'Nobody sees us, nobody knows us.' How you turn things upside down! -- Is the potter not better than the clay, Does something made say of its maker, 'He didn't make me'? Does the product say of its producer, 'He has no discernment'?" (29:9-16)

"For this is a rebellious people; they are lying children, children who refuse to hear the Torah of ADONAI. They say to the seers, 'Do not see!' to those who have visions, 'Do not tell us the visions you have as they really are; but flatter us, fabricate illusions! Get out of the way! Leave the path! Rid us of the Holy One of Isra'el!'

"Therefore here is what the Holy One of Isra'el says; 'Because you reject this word, trust in extortion and rely on deceit, this sin will become for you a crack bulging out high on a wall, showing signs it is ready to fall; then suddenly, all at once, it breaks." (30:9-13)

"Come close, you nations, and listen! Pay close attention, you peoples! Let the earth hear, and everything in it; the world, with all it produces. For ADONAI is angry at every nation, furious with all their armies; he has completely destroyed them, handed them over to slaughter. Their slain will be thrown out, the stench will rise from their corpses, the mountains will flow with their blood. The whole host of heaven will decompose, the heavens themselves be rolled up like a scroll; all their array will wither away like a withering grape-leaf that falls from a vine or a withered fig from a fig tree." (34:1-4)

"Thus says ADONAI, Israel's King and Redeemer, ADONAI-Tzva'ot: 'I am the first, and I am the last; besides me there is no god. Who is like me? Let him speak out! Let him show me clearly what has been happening since I set up the eternal people; let him foretell future signs and events. **Don't be frightened, don't be afraid -- Didn't I tell you this long ago? I foretold it, and you are my witnesses. Is there any god besides me? There is no other Rock -- I know of none."** *(44:6-8)*

"Assemble, come and gather together, you refugees from the nations! Those carrying their wooden idols are ignorant, they pray to a god that cannot save. Let them stand and present their case! Indeed, let them take counsel together. **Who foretold this long ago, announced it in times gone by? Wasn't it I,**

ADONAI? There is no other god besides me, a just G-d and a Savior; there is none besides me. Look to me, and be saved, all the ends of the earth! For I am G-d; there is no other. In the name of myself I have sworn, from my mouth has rightly gone out, a word that will not return -- that to me every knee will bow and every tongue will swear about me that only in ADONAI are justice and strength. All who rage against him will come to him ashamed, but all the descendants of Isra'el will find justice and glory in ADONAI." (45:20-25)

"Seek ADONAI while he is available, call on him while he is still nearby. Let the wicked person abandon his way and the evil person his thoughts; let him return to ADONAI, and he will have mercy on him; let him return to our G-d, for he will freely forgive." (55:6, 7)

"Observe justice, do what is right, for my salvation is close to coming, my righteousness to being revealed. Happy is the person who does this, anyone who grasps it firmly, who keeps Shabbat and does not profane it, and keeps himself from doing any evil." (56:1, 2)

"AND THE FOREIGNERS who join themselves to ADONAI to serve him, to love the name of ADONAI, and to be his workers, ALL WHO KEEP SHABBAT AND DO NOT PROFANE IT, and hold fast to my covenant, I will bring them to my holy mountain and make them joyful in my house of prayer; their burnt offerings and sacrifices will be accepted on my altar; for my house will be called a house of prayer for all peoples." (56:6, 7)

"If you hold back your foot on Shabbat from pursuing your own interests on my holy day; if you call Shabbat a delight, **ADONAI'S HOLY DAY,** worth honoring; then honor it by not doing your usual things or pursuing your interests or speaking about them. If you do, you will find delight in ADONAI -- I will make you ride on the heights of the land and feed you with the heritage of your ancestor Ya'akov, for the mouth of ADONAI has spoken." (58:13, 14)

"Why is your apparel red, your clothes like someone treading a winepress? I have trodden the winepress alone; from the peoples, not one was with me. So I trod them in my anger, *trampled them in my fury; so their lifeblood spurted out on my clothing, and I have stained all my garments; for the day of vengeance that was in my heart and my year of redemption have come. I looked, but there was no one to help, and I was appalled that no one upheld me. Therefore my own arm brought me salvation, and my own fury upheld me. In my anger I trod down the peoples, made them drunk with my fury, then poured out their lifeblood on the earth." (63:2-6)*

"All of us are like someone unclean, all our righteous deeds like menstrual rags; we wither, all of us, like leaves; and our misdeeds blow us away like the wind. No one calls on your name or bestirs himself to take hold of you, for you have hidden your face from us and caused our misdeeds to destroy us. But now, ADONAI, you are our father; we are the clay, you are our potter; and we are all the work of your hands." (64:6-8)

"The kind of person on whom I look with favor is one with a poor and humble spirit, who trembles at my word. Those others might as well kill a person as an ox, as well break a dog's neck as sacrifice a lamb, as well offer pig's blood as offer a grain offering, as well bless an idol as burn incense; Just as these have chosen their ways and enjoy their disgusting practices, so I will enjoy making fools of them, and bring on them the very things they fear. For when I called, no one answered; when I spoke, they did not hear. Instead they did what was evil in my sight and chose what did not please me.'

"Hear the word of ADONAI, you who tremble at his word: 'Your brothers, who hate you and reject you because of my name, have said: 'Let ADONAI be glorified, so we can see your joy.' But they will be put to shame.' that uproar in the city, that sound from the temple, is the sound of ADONAI repaying his foes what they deserve." (66:2-6)

"For -- look! -- ADONAI will come in fire, and his chariots will be like the whirlwind, to render his anger furiously, his rebuke with blazing fire. For ADONAI will judge all humanity with fire and with the sword, and those slain by ADONAI will be many. Those who consecrate and purify themselves in order to enter the gardens, then follow the one who was already there, eating pig meat, reptiles and mice, will all be destroyed

*together,' says ADONAI, 'For I know their deeds and their thoughts. **The time is coming when I will gather together all nations and languages. They will come and see my glory."** (66:15-18)*

"Every month on Rosh-Hodesh and every week on Shabbat, everyone living will come to worship in my presence,' says ADONAI. 'As they leave, they will look on the corpses of the people who rebelled against me. For their worm will never die, and their fire will never be quenched; but they will be abhorrent to all humanity." (66:23, 24)

And YHVH does this for no nation or group of people. He does all this for the sake of his Holy name. For he is a covenant keeping G-d and will fulfill his promises. Let him who has ears, hear what the Spirit of G-d says to the nations.

America's only hope is to follow Nineveh's example when Jonah first warned them. T'shuva! Otherwise, just as Nineveh forgot her roots and the G-d of her salvation, only to have G-d's promise of judgment for her rebellion come upon her head, likewise, America will meet the same fate as spelled out by Nachum:

"(America) is like a pool whose water ebbs away. 'Stop! Stop!' But none of it goes back. Plunder the silver! Plunder the gold! There is no end to the treasure, weighed down with precious things. She is void, vacant; she is made bare. Hearts are melting, knees are knocking; every stomach is churning, every face is drained of color.

"What has become of the lion's den, the cave where the young lions fed, where lion and lioness walked with their cubs, and no one made them afraid? The lion would tear up food for his cubs and strangle prey for his lionesses; he used to fill his caves with prey, his lairs with torn flesh.

"'I am against you,' says ADONAI-Tzva'ot. 'Her chariots I will send up in smoke, the sword will consume your lion cubs, I will destroy your prey from the earth, and your envoys' voices will be heard no more.'

"Woe to the city of blood, steeped in lies, full of prey, with no end to the plunder! The crack of the whip! The rattle of wheels! Galloping horses, jolting chariots, cavalry charging,

swords flashing, spears glittering -- and hosts of slain, heaps of bodies; there is no end to the corpses; they stumble over their corpses.

"*Because of the continual whoring of this whore, this alluring mistress of sorcery, who sells nations with her whoring and families with her sorcery; I am against you,' says ADONAI-Tzva'ot. 'I will uncover your skirts on your face; I will show the nations your private parts and the kingdoms your shame. I will pelt you with disgusting filth, disgrace you and make a spectacle of you. Then all who see you will recoil from you; they will say, '(America) is destroyed!' Who will mourn for her? Where can I find people to comfort you?'*

"*Are you any better than No-Ammon, located among the streams of the Nile, with water all around her, the flood her wall of defense? Ethiopia and Egypt gave her boundless strength, Put and Luvim were there to help you. Still she went captive into exile, her infants torn to pieces at every street corner. Lots were drawn for her nobles, and all her great men were bound in chains.*

"*You too, (America), will be drunk; your senses completely overcome. You too will seek a refuge from the enemy. All your fortifications will be like fig trees with early ripening figs; the moment they are shaken, they fall into the mouth of the eater.*

"*Look at your troops! They behave like women! Your country's gates are wide open to your foes; fire has consumed their bars. Draw water for the siege! Strengthen your fortifications! Go down in the clay, tread the mortar, Take hold of the mold for bricks! There the fire will burn you up; and the sword will cut you down; it will devour you like grasshoppers.*

"*Make yourselves as many as grasshoppers, Make yourselves as many as locusts! You had more merchants than stars in the sky. The locust sheds its skin and flies away. Your guards are like grasshoppers, your marshals like swarms of locusts, which settle on the walls on a cold day, but when the sun rises they fly away; they vanish to no one knows where.*

"*Your shepherds are slumbering, (America), Your leaders are asleep. Your people are scattered all over the mountains, with no one to round them up. Your wound cannot be healed.*

Your injury is fatal. Everyone hearing the news about you claps his hands in joy over you. For who has not been overwhelmed by your relentless cruelty?" (Nachum/Nahum 2:8-3:19)

Who knows? Maybe our nation will repent and find grace in G-d's eye and avoid a great fall. But let us not live in denial and whitewash the truth. G-d is just and holy. He will not be mocked. Remember, no nation is exempt.

"At one time, I may speak about uprooting, breaking down and destroying a nation or kingdom; but if that nation turns from their evil, which prompted me to speak against it, then I relent concerning the disaster I had planned to inflict on it. Similarly, at another time, I may speak about building and planting a nation or kingdom; but if it behaves wickedly from my perspective and doesn't listen to what I say, then I change my mind and don't do the good I said I would do that would have helped it." (Yirmeyahu/Jeremiah 18:7-10)

Alleluia!

Kodesh! Kodesh! Kodesh!

Holy! Holy! Holy!

Is the Lord G-d Almighty1

"We thank you, ADONAI,
G-d of heaven's armies,
the One who is and was,
that you have taken your power
and have begun to rule.
The Goyim raged.
But now your rage has come,
the time for the dead to be judged,
the time for rewarding your servants the prophets
and your holy people,
those who stand in awe of your name,
both small and great.
It is also the time for destroying
those who destroy the earth."
- (Revelation 11:16-18)

Believer. Do not equate the demise of America with the coming of the Messiah. G-d is truly judging this nation as he is all nations. The timing is in his hands. But, the return of the

Messiah will not be at the time of America's fall or destruction. Do not read into these words above that which they do not say.

The Apostasy and the revealing of the Lawless one must take place before his return. When that occurs, will be made known when it happens and not before. But rest assured, America's collapse is not the sign of his return. Neither does America's fall mean your personal demise. If death comes upon us, so be it. We have the blessed hope of a resurrection to look forward to. If we survive, then G-d isn't through with us yet. Get your eyes on Yeshua and get about your Father's business.

"Rejoice in union with the Lord always! I will say it again: rejoice! Let everyone see how reasonable and gentle you are. The Lord is near! Don't worry about anything; on the contrary, make your requests known to G-d by prayer and petition, with thanksgiving. Then G-d's shalom, passing all understanding, will keep your hearts and minds safe in union with the Messiah Yeshua. In conclusion, brothers, focus your thoughts on what is true, noble, righteous, pure, lovable or admirable, on some virtue or on something praiseworthy. Keep doing what you have learned and received from me, what you have heard and seen me doing; then the G-d who gives shalom will be with you." (Philippians 4:4-9)

Remember these words of exhortation from Paul. And recall that they come from him while he resided in prison for his faith in Messiah. And he eventually died for his faith, loving not his life unto death. Follow his example, as he followed Messiah.

G-d is great and greatly to be praised! Alleluia! Bless His name!

Baruch atah ADONAI! Baruch ha shem ADONAI!

Sh'ma Yisrael (and America), ADONAI eloheinu, ADONAI echad. Baruch shem k'vod mal-khoo-to l'olam vaed. Yeshua, ha Mashiach, hoo ADONAI!

LaVergne, TN USA
08 April 2010
178541LV00002B/1/P